Advance Praise for Tr

"Father Joe Classen has sco   ...wisdom and has cast his line deep in the stream of the Word. The result is some real trophies of truth that now grace the walls of the pages you hold!"

STEVE CHAPMAN
CHRISTIAN OUTDOORS AUTHOR

"Father Joe does it again! I really enjoyed the way he combines the spirit of the outdoors to the bonding with the Lord. I tell you, I enjoyed the excitement of the hunting stories; it made me feel I was right there with him! I would recommend this book to anyone who loves the outdoors and wants to understand the love that God has for us and his creation that we love to share the woods with."

DAN YOUNG
HOST OF *OUTDOORS TRADITIONS TV*
AND THE RADIO SHOW *OUTDOORS WITH OUTDOORS DAN*

"Along with reflecting on his hunting pursuits, Father Classen balances a mixture of fishing adventures in the 'Great Land' of America's last frontier and a faith reflection on the meaning of life, to which the extravagant beauty of such places as Alaska points. Father Classen both entertains us and instructs our faith with this interesting and enlightening read, which gives substance from a Catholic/Christian perspective to those who find God in their experiences of nature."

MOST REV. ROGER SCHWIETZ, O.M.I.
ARCHBISHOP OF ANCHORAGE

Tracking Virtue, Conquering Vice

TRACKING VIRTUE, CONQUERING VICE

A Guide for Spiritual Survival

REV. JOSEPH F. CLASSEN

Our Sunday Visitor Publishing Division
Our Sunday Visitor, Inc.
Huntington, Indiana 46750

Copyright © 2009 by Our Sunday Visitor Publishing Division, Our Sunday Visitor, Inc. Published 2009

14 13 12 11 10 09   1 2 3 4 5 6 7 8 9

Our Sunday Visitor Publishing Division
Our Sunday Visitor, Inc.
200 Noll Plaza
Huntington, IN 46750

ISBN: 978-1-59276-476-1 (Inventory No. T713)
LCCN: 2008937151

Cover design: Tyler Ottinger
Cover photo: Design Pics
Interior design: Sherri L. Hoffman
Interior photos: Rev. Joseph F. Classen

PRINTED IN THE UNITED STATES OF AMERICA

Contents

Envy and the undertow of ingratitude. Fraternal charity: An attitude of gratitude.

Acknowledgments

First and foremost, thanks be to God for filling my soul with an unquenchable, indestructible, passionate love of his awe-inspiring creation and the tremendous privilege of sharing his life, love, and truth with others.

As always, I'd like to offer my heartfelt thanks to all those wonderful, incredibly hospitable folks who have invited me along on outdoor adventures, allowed me to spend time on their property, and provided me with a setting to hunt for God and fish for the Lord.

My sincere thanks to my family and friends who have been so motivating over all these years. I'd like to offer a word of gratitude to those who have assisted in this project with their literary and creative talents (especially Lynne Lang), to my brother priests and the bishops who have been of great support, and to those in the outdoor industry who have offered their kind words of encouragement.

Another special word of thanks must be given to Kathy Etling for taking the time to write the Foreword for this book in the midst of her many other projects.

Last, but certainly not least, I'd like to offer a big round of applause for all the great folks at Our Sunday Visitor, who have been such a joy to work with.

God bless you all!

Fr. Joe Classen

DEDICATION

Father Joe and Eugene Kopp

THIS BOOK IS DEDICATED in loving memory of Eugene James Kopp (October 24, 1940 — January 24, 2007). Gene was one of the most wonderful human beings I have ever met. I'll never forget his deep, sincere, devoted love of God, family, and friends. His inspiring admiration of the great outdoors and the humbling gratitude he expressed for the beautiful magnificence of our Lord's gift of nature was a quality that bonded our providential friendship . . . which was far too short.

I logged many hours at the Kopp farm, talking about life, watching the sun setting over the rich Missouri landscape, listening to the wisdom of "Grandma" (Gene's 106-year-old mother), whistling back to the quail, admiring the wildlife, and feasting on the best barbecued pork steaks and potato salad on planet Earth!

I miss you terribly, Gene. Please save a spot for me on the front porch of heaven, my friend.

FR. JOE CLASSEN

Foreword

WHEN QUESTIONED, hunters and anglers will often profess a love of and appreciation for the great outdoors that goes well beyond that felt by ordinary citizens, even those who enjoy wilderness activities like mountain biking, birding, or hiking. But the wonder expressed by hunters and anglers sometimes goes even further than mere love and appreciation. It's rather common to hear outdoors men and women mentioning how close they feel to God, as they trudge across fields and forests in search of wild game, wait long hours in tree stands, or wade in or boat on streams and lakes in the hope that fish will strike the offerings tied to the ends of their lines.

Why is it that some of us can feel this closeness to God — and will even crave God's closeness — while others expend their energy debating or denying God's existence? Indeed, it's become fashionable to do the latter, as has denigrating the intelligence of any person or group whose faith in the existence of Almighty God and his Son, Jesus Christ, is strong and unwavering.

And yet, researchers have discovered that seeking God and hoping to find him could very well be hardwired into our human nature by way of the brain. Scientists who delve into the mysteries of this organ recently identified a region they've dubbed the "God spot," because it generates a noticeably greater amount of electrical current when certain people, whose brains are being scanned by EEGs, are asked to think about God.

Not all of the participants have an active God spot, and so the question that has researchers scrambling for answers is: Why do even a few human brains, much less a large percentage, reveal such an overload of specialized electrical activity at the very thought of their God? Or this one: Are all people born with a God spot that, in some, eventually atrophies from disuse over time? The latter question, of course, seems more appropriate, given God's love for us — a love so great that he sent his only Son down from heaven to suffer and die for us so that we, his human children, would be saved from our sins.

For more than a century, scientists have theorized that the Earth's creatures evolved over time in ways that allowed the fittest of each species to survive and occupy its particular niche in nature. The mechanism that is thought to drive evolution is genetic mutation. Each slight change in genetic makeup could make a particular individual better suited for survival than others of its kind. If that was so, the theory goes, that individual would then survive to pass on its superior genetic traits to its offspring.

So why would any member of *Homo sapiens* — a species that stands alone at the top of the food chain by virtue of its vast intellect, opposable thumbs, altruistic nature, and a free will that sends humans searching for answers to the great questions of our time (questions that in some instances have yet to be asked) — possess such a God spot? What conceivable survival advantage could a God spot bestow upon a human being? And when, during human evolution, did such a God spot appear?

It has been said that nature abhors a vacuum. Or, perhaps, it's God, not nature, who abhors a vacuum. Thus, the God spot. It is thought that our earliest human ancestors climbed down from the trees in the jungles of Africa and made their way to the savannas, where, over the course of myriad generations, they became one of the world's dominant creatures. A great migration then began. As waves of early human migrants ventured into regions of the world vastly different from the place in which they had originated, the color of their eyes, hair, and skin soon began to change or evolve, along with other morphological details, the better to adapt to new climates and geography.

But why did early humans evolve a God spot, if evolve it they did? Were the first female and male to possess such God spots Adam and Eve? And did God bestow upon them their God spots when he gave them their immortal souls, thus forever setting them and us apart from the other animals? Is that how God created us, his children, "in his own image" (Gen 1:27), by endowing us with an innate ability to seek, know, love, and serve him so that we could someday join him in heaven?

Could it also be possible that the "original sin" which caused humankind's downfall was the same pride that sent Lucifer, once God's favorite, plunging into hell? Could pride have caused Adam and Eve to deny God's very being, as the God of everyone and everything, just as so many so-called sophisticates or members of the intelligentsia deny it today?

We know the God spot functioned in the brains of many early humans, and we have seen evidence of the stirring of their souls in ancient sites of religious significance that have been found throughout the world. Cultural anthropologists and archaeologists have told us that early humans — and even their close cousins, the Neanderthals — believed in a life after death, because they buried, burned, or preserved amulets, tokens, and offerings along with the bodies of their dead.

We know that many of them also believed in the divine, because their artwork crudely depicted images representing powerful gods and goddesses who, they hoped, would exert an influence on people and the natural world that might benefit them. People from all corners of the globe have always sought God. So many have done so throughout the ages, in fact, that researchers continue to search for physical clues as to why God always seems to have been so important to us.

As an outdoors writer, I've talked with many of today's outdoors men and women, who come from all walks of life. Rarely do I ever encounter one who does not believe in God or some higher power. Outdoors men and women see firsthand the wonders of nature and the glories of the world that are all around them. Few, judging from my personal observation, seem to possess the hubris to believe that everything they behold, starting with the universe, was initiated by a random "big bang" that astronomers admit would have resulted in eons of chaos on an unfathomable scale. Could such incredible order as exists today really have come about by mere chance, or is it part of Someone's grand plan?

Thank goodness for Father Joe Classen and books like *Tracking Virtue, Conquering Vice: A Guide for Spiritual Survival.* Father Joe, who serves as a parish priest in the Archdiocese of St. Louis, is a priest first, a hunter and an angler second. He's a devout Catholic, one who answered the call of God when he was very young and embraced his vocation as a priest.

Father Joe, a priest very much like each person who will read this book, is also different from most of us. Father Joe works each day to lead parishioners and readers alike to the Way, the Truth, and the Life on a path that each of us can relate to. He firmly believes that the trail best taken to reach this destination is one that traverses fields and forests, lakes and waterways.

Father Joe firmly believes that we can find God, and know him more fully, through hunting and fishing. In his books, Father Joe always explains how these very activities — outdoor pursuits beloved by so many of us — will help us discover ways to better understand, obey, and love God the Father, God the Son, and God the Holy Spirit. Father Joe's first book, *Hunting for God, Fishing for the Lord: Encountering the Sacred in the Great Outdoors*, provides an excellent template for anyone who occasionally wonders about life and its meaning. It includes confessions of some of Father's own personal quirks and foibles, together with anecdotes relating disastrous excursions that will ring true to anyone who's ever hunted or fished. Father Joe also explains his own personal philosophy, as it relates to his outdoor experiences, some of which border on the downright hilarious. Of course, what would you expect from someone so enamored of bowhunting that he set up a personal archery range on his parish rectory's second floor?

In his latest book, Father Joe provides important historical information about Jesus Christ and evidence of his life, while also relating many of the prophecies that foretold his coming. He discusses free will and faith, virtue and vice. And he does it all in a way that will tempt you to stay up all night, reading his book from cover to cover. But that, dear reader, would be a disservice to yourself. *Tracking Virtue, Conquering Vice* was written to be savored. Each sentence, each page, each anecdote, could easily stand on its own merits, to be sure. But each also provides much more than what can be easily gleaned by skimming over its surface, whether one is reading the exciting adventure of Father Joe's first archery hunt for bull elk or the all-too-common appearance of two inner vices — greed and envy — when his bowhunting companion, and not Father Joe, bagged a trophy whitetail buck not far from where Father Joe had been waiting on stand.

Like most hunters and fishermen, Father Joe finds solace in the natural world around him, and even evidence of God's existence. He sometimes gets angry with God, something that anyone who's ever dealt with adversity in large servings will certainly be able to understand. But Father Joe also walks his readers through the aftermath of those times when his actions have later caused him to look back with shame and regret. Who hasn't found himself or herself feeling the same way? And how many of us have known how to deal with it or how to make it right?

Father Joe serves as a friendly guide for readers, as they examine the circumstances of their own lives or find common ground in his various outdoor experiences. And he's able to do so without seeming preachy or, God forbid, "holier than thou," as some people are so fond of whining. He does so by example, by revealing the faults and vices that lurk within his own soul, while referring always to his own life experiences to illustrate how each of us might prevail over our own moral low points.

When you finish reading *Tracking Virtue, Conquering Vice*, you will walk away knowing more about God the Father, God the Son, and God the Holy Spirit than you've ever known before. You'll understand more about yourself, your hopes and dreams, your vices and virtues, and even what makes you tick. Best of all, you will walk away after having been entertained by a master storyteller, an everyman who's dedicated his life to serving God and — whether shepherding his parish flock or writing about his outdoor adventures — leading others to do the same.

Tracking Virtue, Conquering Vice is a remarkable book on all levels. Every Catholic, every Christian, every hunter, and every angler will enjoy Father Joe Classen's wonderful book.

KATHY ETLING

Kathy Etling lives in Osage Beach, Missouri, with her husband, Bob, after having been born and raised in St. Louis County. As an adult, she resided for decades in that same county and lived the entire time within a mile of St. Margaret Mary Alacoque Church, Father Joe's present parish assignment.

She has been an outdoors writer for more than a quarter century, and is currently the outdoors reporter for the St. Louis Post-Dispatch *and a field editor for* Petersen's Bowhunting *magazine.*

She is the author of 10 books, including The Quotable Cowboy, Cougar Attacks: Encounters of the Worst Kind, *and the best-selling outdoors book* Hunting Superbucks: How to Hunt Trophy Mule and Whitetail Deer.

Kathy credits her wonderful Catholic education — at St. Michael the Archangel School in Shrewsbury and Kirkwood's Ursuline Academy — with providing her with the tools needed to excel in the field of outdoors writing and the business of life.

Introduction

THE HUNT CONTINUES

Father Joe is ready to go!

GREETINGS, FRIENDS! Well, here we are again, hunting for God and fishing for the Lord. I must confess that I originally began this project with no intention of it actually becoming a complete book. During the time I was putting the finishing touches on my second book, *Meat & Potatoes Catholicism*, I found myself writing just as a way to wind down in the evenings. But what I found myself writing about were more topics of spirituality and the great outdoors! Funny how I just naturally gravitate toward those things! Let me tell you right now, folks: The Lord has blessed me with some spectacular, incredible, and amazing hunting and fishing adventures during the last few years, and you'll be hearing all about them in this volume. I have no doubt that these experiences are blessings that I have been given to share with you, the reader. And I can't wait to share them with you!

Since my first book, *Hunting for God, Fishing for the Lord*, I've made a lot of new friends from all walks of life, from all different faith traditions, and from all over the country. I've even had the great privilege of getting together with some of these good people to hunt and fish. It's been an immense joy to hear from all of you and to share in the excitement of your spiritual and outdoor adventures. I look forward to more.

To set the stage for the material presented in this book, let me start by saying that while I'm certainly not bashful about my priesthood and my Catholic faith, I do make a conscious effort to keep my outdoor-inspired spiritual writing appealing and applicable to people of all faith traditions, and even to those who perhaps have little or no faith at all — at least not yet! So, in other words, this is meant to be an "ecumenical" book. As a Christian, I prefer to focus on what we all have in common, instead of bitterly arguing and squabbling over the misunderstandings and doctrinal differences that may still divide us to varying degrees. If you can read the following prayer/creed and agree with what is being said, then guess what? At least for starters, we're on the same team:

> I believe in God, the Father almighty, creator of heaven and earth; and in Jesus Christ, his only Son, our Lord; who was conceived by the Holy Spirit, born of the Virgin Mary, suffered under Pontius Pilate, was crucified, died, and was buried. He descended to the dead; the third day he arose again from the dead. He ascended into heaven and sits at the right hand of God, the Father almighty; from thence he shall come to judge the living and the dead. I believe in the Holy Spirit, the holy catholic [which means "universal"] Church, the communion of saints, the forgiveness of sins, the resurrection of the body, and life everlasting. Amen.

As I mentioned, one does not necessarily have to be a person of faith to enjoy, appreciate, and learn from the material presented in this book. No matter who you are, no matter where you are on the journey of life, no matter if you don't even particularly enjoy the outdoors, there is something in these pages that will be of value for you. In the grand scheme of things, this book really has little to do with the outdoors — but at the same time, the reader will get a double-barreled dose of action-packed adventure. So for those of you who do not hunt or fish, and who question the ethics of such pursuits, please take a moment and read about the ethics of hunting and fishing, found in the Appendix in the back of this book.

In *Hunting for God*, I covered a wide variety of spiritual topics. But in this installment, I will be zeroing in on more specific areas. So along with loads of outdoor excitement and a fair dose of humor, we'll be looking at three main themes or concepts: "tracking God," the "seven deadly sins" and their remedy virtues, and finally "spiritual survival."

Why these topics? First, mankind is on the *hunt* for God as never before. As our culture continues to bombard us with the lies of atheism, materialism, secularism, and relativism, a hunger for the truth and the divine is emerging quite prominently. Unfortunately, many are seeking to satisfy that hunger by consuming even more garbage, which is disguised and marketed with the term "spirituality." As I've said before, "spirituality" is not necessarily about engaging in things that entertain us or make us feel good. True spirituality is that which leads us into communion and fellowship with the one and only Spirit: the Holy Spirit. It is that which brings about real, positive change in our lives and enables us to produce good fruit. And make no mistake: Bringing these things about is not always a cakewalk! It requires dedication, commitment, discipline, and most importantly, the love and the grace of God. More about all that later.

Secondly, I chose to focus on virtue and vice as the main staples of this book simply because our society, and quite often our very lives, are in a "vice-grip," if you will, of the destructive power of sin and vice. This, too, is manufactured and marketed to us, and it is blatantly crammed down our throats on a daily basis. Lust-producing themes and images run wild and saturate mass-media advertising and entertainment. What does an image of a more-than-half-naked lady in a sexually explicit position have to do with selling beer in the grocery store? You got me! But we see it, and much worse, every day. Overdriven sexual imagery is shoved in our faces at every turn. Is it any wonder that the numbers of STDs, teen pregnancies, sex crimes, and condom sales have skyrocketed? Prolific sin historically precedes the downfall of a culture — and I dare say that we are teetering dangerously on the edge!

Not a day goes by that we are not subjected to vice. Wrathful anger and gratuitous violence are celebrated in the music, movies, and video games of our young people, yet we're baffled when a troubled youth goes to school and guns down his classmates. Our multimillion-dollar media moguls are quick to reject any blame for society's moral deterioration and simply say that troubled relationships, failed upbringings, and mental illness are to blame for things like criminal teen violence. But can one deny that when a troubled youth spends hours a day on his computer, month after month, diligently carrying out conscious, methodical acts of unbelievable virtual violence, that there is not going to be an extremely severe negative influence? Insanity!

Our culture trains us in the ways of vice. As I heard a speaker recently point out, we are afraid to let our sisters/daughters/wives walk down the street alone because we know good and well what monsters, created by our vice, lurk around the next corner.

In our daily experience, the vices of pride and greed shout out to us, "You deserve the best! Get more!" Weeks later, when the credit cards are maxed out and one's debt is through the roof, "the best" and "more" don't seem like such great ideas after all. Gluttonous "all you can eat" buffets and "supersized" meals may come cheap and are readily available, but the ravaging of one's health from obesity commands a very high price indeed.

We've all heard of the "seven deadly sins" over the years. Famous artists — such as Giotto, Lorenzetti, Bosch, and Brueghel — have portrayed these vices in paintings. We hear about them in literary masterpieces such as Chaucer's *Canterbury Tales* and Dante's *Divine Comedy*. These seven vices have even been the subject of movies, such as the 1967 comedy *Bedazzled,* starring Dudley Moore and Peter Cook. I would dare say, though, that many of us probably have no idea where the notion of the original seven deadly sins came from or how the Church's teaching about them developed. This being the case, let's take a quick look at the history of them.

The seven deadly sins actually go all the way back to the first century of Eastern monasticism and were the basis for a list of vices that were harmful to this way of life. As time went on, St. Gregory the Great (in the sixth century) used these as the basis for the "capital sins," which are the roots from which other sinful behaviors come. Later, St. Thomas Aquinas (in the 13th century) added that these seven are not necessarily sins in and of themselves but more the dispositions toward sin; they are that which initiate a habit of sinfulness and foster a severe threat to that which is morally good.

Over the centuries, the exact list of the seven sins/vices continued to go through a bit of rehashing and debate. But eventually, pride, greed, envy, wrath, gluttony, lust, and sloth became the standard. Along with the Ten Commandments, the list of the seven deadly sins/vices became a common device for doing an examination of one's conscience — not a bad idea for us today, either.

We'll get to more of this later. But for now, let's get on with our hunting for God and fishing for the Lord!

Chapter 1

TRACKING GOD

IF YOU'RE READING THIS SENTENCE right now, you obviously have eyes. But let me ask you: Can you truly see? You may have vision, but do you have the ability to harness and focus that vision to seek out particular objects and minuscule details, and gather information that would otherwise go unseen and unknown? Let's try a little demonstration: Right now I'm going to stop typing for a moment and take a look out my window. . . .

All right, I'm back, and here is my report: I saw a kid playing basketball in the parking lot across the way, and I also saw the neighbors' houses, their cars, several trees and bushes, mailboxes, and that's about it. That is all I perceived by means of my vision from an initial look. Now, I'm going to go back and truly exercise my power to see. . . .

Okay, I've returned once again, and this time I have much more to report. You know that kid I mentioned who was playing basketball? Well, he had on some ratty, black Nike shorts; white, dirt-stained, Adidas shoes; short, rather ridiculous-looking athletic socks; a torn-up red tank top with his school logo on it and the number 4 on the back. He was about 5 feet 5 inches tall, probably 155 pounds, and looked kind of like a spoiled-rotten punk! (Just kidding. He's a good kid.)

Remember those houses I mentioned? It turns out that one was a well-worn, two-story place made of brick; another was a newer-looking, single-story house with white siding; and the third was the same as the second one, except it had cedar siding. The trees I saw were one fine specimen of a dogwood, four red maples, one Bradford pear (complete with an abundance of underdeveloped fruit), five short-leaf pines (which appeared to be struggling to stay alive), and two white oaks. Halfway up the one oak was a skinny gray squirrel cutting away on an acorn, and the maples had a mockingbird and two plump robins flying about. Around those bushes — which, by the way, were Nannyberry bushes — were two rather chubby, lazy-looking cottontail rabbits. There was a white Ford Explorer with a cracked back taillight, a red GMC Canyon, and a burgundy-colored Ford Escort out there. The numbers on those mailboxes were 243, 244, and 245 — and number 244 was caved in from what looked to be the work of a midnight mailbox basher. I have no doubt that I could fill the rest of this entire book with details of things I saw from that second viewing and what they tell me, or imply. But you get the point.

You see, we often do not see. We take many things for granted and simply glance over vast amounts of information and data in the blink of an eye. Everything we see tells a story and can lead to the discovery and solving of an endless multitude of mysteries.

One of my favorite things to do when I'm in the woods is to walk along a damp creek bed and have a look at the various animal tracks. On any given day, I'll have no problem finding deer tracks, raccoon tracks, great blue heron tracks, turkey tracks, coyote tracks, and many others. By studying those tracks closer, I can tell how big the animals are and whether they have been there recently or came through days earlier.

The Master Tracker

Imagine that one could look at a track and tell if the animal was male or female; if it had any injuries; exactly what time of day it came by; if it was hungry, pregnant, nervous, calm, moving fast or slow; where it was headed; if it stopped to look right, left, up, down, or paused to get a drink. Imagine that one could answer every conceivable question about an animal from looking at its tracks. Impossible, right? Well, there is at least one person who can do just that. His name is Tom Brown, Jr., and he is a master tracker who was taught this incredible skill by an Apache Indian. In the motion picture *The Hunted*, actor Tommy Lee Jones plays the part of a professional tracker whose character is based on Tom Brown.

Mr. Brown is the author of many books, and he runs a nature, tracking, and wilderness-survival school. As far-fetched and as inconceivable as his almost miraculous ability may sound, it is the real deal. He has tracked down hundreds of lost outdoor enthusiasts, fugitives, and dangerous animals in instances where police, helicopters, and bloodhounds have failed. In his book *The Science and Art of Tracking*, Mr. Brown discusses and teaches an approach to his almost unbelievable, yet very real, tracking skills. It all comes down to putting in the "dirt time" — and lots and lots of it! It's a matter of studying, with mind-blowing attention to detail, the most intricate characteristics of tracks and "pressure releases" (as he calls them) of an animal or human. But the real key is developing a potent, harnessed awareness and a vision that goes far beyond just looking at the ground: it's a matter of truly seeing. Tom has mastered this so well that he claims to be able to literally track mice across gravel — and from the research I've done on the man, I don't doubt it.

In my book *Meat & Potatoes Catholicism*, there is a chapter where I talk about the experience of coming across the tracks and signs of the biggest buck I'd ever encountered in the wild. Although I never saw him until months later, I knew he was there. I simply had no doubt at all as to that deer's existence. To somehow convince myself that his huge tracks, that the massive rubs he was making on trees, and that the gigantic scrapes he left everywhere were some kind of a hoax or deception would have been utter nonsense. But technically, without seeing and later getting a photograph of that incredible buck, I could not have *proven* to you that he did, in fact, exist. And even then, one might have said that I was hallucinating or that those pictures were doctored.

Tracking God With Philosophy, Theology, and Science

As far back as recorded history goes, and for as long as rational man has walked the earth, he has searched for God. He has desperately tried to prove God's existence. Man has never ceased attempting to track down the Almighty. One could fill an entire library with books and intellectual debates over God's existence. There is the ontological argument, the teleological argument, the cosmological argument for God's existence, and a ton of other obscure-sounding terms that intellectuals, philosophers, theologians, and scientists have debated over and wrestled with for centuries, right up to this very day. Many a sharply honed, devastatingly brilliant mind has been put through the ringer and pushed to the edge of (and sometimes into) madness in this pursuit of proving that God is, in fact, "out there" — or, that he is, without a shadow of a doubt, not there.

His tracks are everywhere!

And when it's all said and done, what is the result of this mental pilgrimage to the temple of reason and proposed truth? The result is shelves upon shelves of books and philosophy classes filled with often bitter yet passionate debates — but still no actual sightings or photographs of the Eternal One. There is still no tangible "proof" that satisfies all. And guess what, folks? There never will be. There are, however, loads of God-sign. He has left his tracks virtually everywhere, and we can come to know him quite profoundly, intimately, and personally by learning to truly see; by reading those tracks with a discerning, trained eye; and most importantly, by an "aware awareness."

One of many brilliant individuals who sought to track God by philosophical and theological means was St. Thomas Aquinas. He came up with what is known as the "five proofs" for God's existence. Like all other intellectual "proofs" that have emerged over the centuries, Aquinas' have been argued over, criticized, and rejected by more than a few. Many a fiery, pencil-necked atheist or agnostic bookworm will shout in defiance, "Logic and reason cannot be trusted! There are no absolutes!" Yet, *they* use logic and reason to actually show that logic and reason cannot be trusted, and that the absolute of "no absolutes" is in fact, well, an absolute! Confused? Don't worry, there will be no tests. Anyhow, getting back to Aquinas' five proofs for the existence of God, they do provide some good food for thought, and they make a decent starting place for this ultimate tracking job of seeking the divine. Let's have a quick look at them.

The first proof for God's existence, according to Aquinas, is achieved by studying motion. From plain and simple observations, we see that an object that is in motion — be it an arrow, a fishing lure, or a fantastically delicious roast beef sandwich being shoved into my mouth — was put in motion by something else: my bow shot the arrow, my fishing rod cast the lure, and my hand put the sandwich into my mouth. But something or someone put my bow, my fishing rod, and my hand in motion — I did, and I am the one who is responsible for the movement of those things. And "I" consists of my body, empowered by my intellect, empowered by my will, empowered by an awareness of my awareness (which is a distinctly human process).

On a larger scale, take a look at something like the planets. They are in motion. Something then had to put them in motion; if it was a "big bang," then something had to light the fuse, something had to make the raw materials to cause that explosion. Nothing can move itself. Every object in motion has a mover. All motion is traced back to an "unmoved" mover — that is, to something or someone who puts things in motion while not being moved itself. Therefore, this initial "unmoved" mover is — following Aquinas' logic — God.

More signs of the Almighty!

Aquinas' second proof is somewhat similar to the first; but instead of dealing with motion, he looks at creation and existence. Here, the idea is that nothing creates itself; nothing brings about its own existence. I didn't bring about my own existence, my parents didn't bring about theirs, and so on and so forth. There is nothing — including anything that regenerates and propagates itself — that is responsible for its own existence. Something or someone (which Aquinas calls God) is responsible for that principle act of being created and coming into existence.

Of course, as we've all thought and pondered since we were 5 years old, the next question is, "Well, then, who made God?" The answer to this, my friends, is quite simple: it's a *mystery* that we will never know the answer to until we meet God. As I mentioned, these "proofs" are merely a starting place for a search that reason, logic, and science will never satisfy. It is a search that can only be fulfilled with faith. More about that later.

Aquinas' third proof talks about "contingent" things and "noncontingent," or "necessary," things. A contingent thing is something that depends on something else for its existence. For example, we human beings depend on air, water, and food to live and exist here on earth. But what about air, water, and food — and, for that matter, everything else? Have these other things always existed, dependent upon nothing else? The answer, says Aquinas, is no, so he then correctly reasons that *everything* is contingent — no exceptions. Therefore, there must be something or someone necessary to cause these contingent things — and according to Aquinas, that necessary something or someone is, you guessed it, God.

Thomas' fourth proof is based on the degrees of perfection. For example, in athletic competitions such as gymnastics, the athletes are judged on their performance. If the gymnast goes through her routine without making any mistakes whatsoever, she will win the event because she has performed a *perfect* routine. Meanwhile, another competitor might embarrassingly fumble and make all sorts of humiliating errors and fail dismally, while spectators viciously ridicule her from the stands! How awful! Thus, we see that there are degrees of perfection. We see this in things, too. Some products are manufactured flawlessly, exactly as they were designed, while others might get damaged during production. And so, there are perfect products and not-so-perfect products. You might have a shirt that fits absolutely impeccably and another that has three sleeves, has the tag in the front, is missing a button, and was purchased at a "factory seconds" store for 50 cents.

Aquinas then points out that for everything — including qualities such as knowledge, goodness, and love — there must be a perfect standard by which they all are measured. This perfection, then, is that of the perfection contained in God.

The fifth proof, and the one that is perhaps the strongest and easiest case of all to understand, is what many refer to today as "intelligent design." This "proof" points out the obvious: that something or someone simply has to be responsible for creating things as we know them. The astounding, mind-boggling complexity of created things, and of the universe at large, is just far too amazing to think that it's all a big cosmic mistake or happenstance. And even though the theory of evolution is still technically a *theory*, could this process be responsible for making perfection out of gas, dirt, proteins, and enzymes, which were just aimlessly floating around out there in space or lying on a beach? And if so, even that process would then have been a perfectly designed one.

Scientists point out that the odds of DNA assembling by chance are 10,000 to 1. Other scientists proclaim that this isn't a matter of "chance," but that it's a combination of the laws of physics, nuclear force, electromagnetism, and gravity. But then, because laws are also things that are created, who is responsible for making these laws that govern the universe? Who would have known that we needed them? Round and round we go! When it's all said and done, once again, what are we left with? We are left with a mystery that we will never solve, a mystery that our feeble brains cannot comprehend or understand, but yet a mystery that divine revelation, faith, and plain common sense solve quite easily.

As a favorite theologian of mine used to say, take a look around the room you're sitting in for a moment. Everything in that room was designed, created, and manufactured based on an idea. The chair you are sitting in was created to give your legs and back a break so that you can be in a more comfortable position to do things like read this book. The glasses on your face or the contacts you may be wearing were created to correct the poor lenses in your eyes. The light bulbs that are illuminating the room were created from an idea to provide light without having to burn a fuel of some kind or rely on the sun. Your house was built in accordance with the ideas of an architect. Without all these ideas, our lives as we know them would be unthinkable and unbearable. The existence that mankind has made for itself is therefore based on the ideas of mankind. Likewise, the existence that God has made for us, and which the entire universe is based on, is his idea.

If you have ever gutted a deer (or any animal for that matter), you most likely had a quick, graphic display of divine ideas. How ingenious! A chunk of meat the size of a fist pumps red liquid into other chunks of meat, which are attached to an agile, flexible, yet strong skeletal system, to enable that deer to see, breathe, smell, hear, run, jump, fight, breed, eat, process food and waste, grow antlers and fur, and give birth. Those same basic elements and chunks of meat that are also part of the human body can do things like paint a masterpiece or play a Mozart symphony, not to mention compose it! And the emotionally moving, beautiful sounds of that symphony can make one laugh, cry, or inspire other ideas that bring about a creation of one's own. Meat playing music? A bunch of flesh, bones, and bloody goo painting the Sistine Chapel? Who would have thought! Can a mere combination of laws or chance bring this about? Can mere bodily machines that are all made of the same basic materials each express themselves so uniquely and truly individually?

Tracking God Through Creation

All of creation tells us something of the one who created it, just as every track tells us something of the animal that stamped it into the dirt. In a likewise fashion, we can know something of people from what they have made and from the ideas that inspired their creation. Works of art — whether music, painting, writing, or custom motorcycle building — can all tell us what psychological, spiritual, emotional, and even physical state the person who created them was in. We can discover an artist's or craftsman's intentions, feelings, thoughts, or proposed agenda by carefully studying his or her masterpiece. Art and craftsmanship of any kind make an intentional — sometimes subtle, sometimes bold — personal statement.

This phenomenon takes place on a much simpler level as well. Walk into someone's home, and you can tell much about the owner from how the surroundings are organized or decorated. Notice how a particular person prepares food, cleans up, or what his or her work ethic is like, and you will discover much about that person. And no matter who that individual is, even if he or she is shrouded in a cloud of mystery and we just can't figure out or learn what makes that person tick, if enough time is spent and if enough careful, detailed observation is implemented, one will eventually discover who and what the person is all about.

The same applies to God. We see the basics of who he is and what he is like from observing and studying his engineering, creation, organization, efficiency, sense of beauty, and even his sense of humor. (For example: Why is it that the ugliest, creepiest things on earth — like a king crab, a halibut, or a big, dirty, mud-sucking catfish — are the tastiest? Mmmmm!)

Indigenous people such as the Native Americans were/are a people with a great connection to the earth, to all of creation, and thus they recognized the obvious role and importance that the Creator played. When studying the spirituality of Native Americans, one will discover a fair amount of diversity in beliefs and practices — but yet, at the same time, there are shared underlying, defining characteristics. Robert Staffanson, of the American Indian Institute, points out a few of these (as quoted in *Sourcebook of the World's Religions: An Interfaith Guide to Religion and Spirituality*, Third Edition, 2008).

First, there is the *"recognition of the interconnectedness of all Creation*, and the responsibility of human beings to use their intelligence in protecting that interconnectedness. This applies particularly to the life-giving elements of water, air, and soil."

Second, there is a *"belief that all life is equal*, and that the presence of the life spark implies a degree of spirituality whether in humans, animals, or plants. In their [Native Americans'] view the species of animals and birds, as well as forests and other plant life, have as much 'right' to existence as human beings, and should not be damaged or destroyed. That does not mean that they cannot be used but that use has limitations."

Third, Staffanson states that their *"primary concern is with the long-term welfare of life* rather than with short-term expediency or comfort. They consider all issues and actions in relationship to their long-term effect on all life, not just human life."

And as a fourth and final point of consideration, their *"spirituality is undergirded by thankfulness to the Creator.* Prayer, ceremonies, meditation and fasting are an important part of their lives. But they ask for nothing. They give thanks for all forms of life and for all the elements that make life possible, and they are concerned with the continuation of that life and the ingredients upon which it depends."

And so it is, like the Native Americans, when one spends countless hours in creation, relying on creation, observing creation, working with creation, respecting creation, and properly using creation, one is able to come to know in a very real way the Creator and enter into a kind of relationship with him. But the next big questions, then, are these: Is that where it ends? Is learning to read the "tracks" of the Creator with the awareness of a master tracker the solution and the way to truly discover God? Is it only by creation, only by acknowledging this childishly obvious "intelligent design," that we come to know the Divine Architect?

The answer is no. Becoming aware of creation is only the very beginning of this tracking job. Acknowledging the fact that everything cannot come from nothing is only a mere step in the right direction.

Tracking God Through History and Divine Revelation

Imagine now that the Creator — the one responsible for all that is, was, and ever will be — actually desired to get to know us, who are made in his image and likeness, on a very personal level. Imagine that he desired to genuinely enter into our world and our lives, and to reveal himself as one of us, but at the same time still hold on to his divine nature. What if the "Great Spirit" actually came down here, walked and talked with us, and told us everything we needed to know to fulfill the purpose for which we were created? What if that entity was willing to enter into the mess we've made for ourselves and repair the eternal damage, which we've caused by means of the evil we have brought into a world that was initially created good? Hence, the person of Jesus Christ takes center stage as the fullness of God's revelation to mankind and the instrument of atonement, reparation, and salvation for all.

At this point, you non-Christian readers will probably roll your eyes and say, "Oh yeah, here we go. I knew it was coming. Now we gotta get thumped over the head with the Bible and listen to all this Jesus stuff!" You might defiantly object and think to yourself: *I don't want to hear it! The Bible is a book of fairy tales, Jesus never existed, and religion is, as Karl Marx said, "the opium of the people."* But before you skip over the rest of this chapter, bear with me for a few pages, and let's see if we can *objectively* "track" Jesus. After all, there is good reason that we make such a big deal out of him.

For starters, we know there are many different world religions. We have Islam, Buddhism, Hinduism, Judaism, Confucianism, and so on. Some feel that all religions basically point to the same goal, and that they all are just different expressions or paths to the same God. Let's take a look at that proposition, using basic theological principles.

As a starting point, for the true, authentic revelation of God to come through a particular individual, and for a religion to be the perfect embodiment of divine truth, that individual must meet three criteria. First, he must be "preannounced." Naturally, if God planned to pay us a visit, he would tell us he was coming so that we would be prepared — it's just common courtesy! Second, an individual who is the embodiment and manifestation of the divine would have to confirm his true divinity with signs and miracles, with things that only God can do. Third, that individual must not teach anything that is contrary to reason or that is self-negating.

When we look at the founding figures of the world's major religions, none but Jesus meets all three criteria. This is, in a nutshell, what the Bible is all about. The Old Testament is about what will be fulfilled in the New Testament, and vice versa. In Scripture, we experience the living Word of God; we come to understand the history and revelation of God and his plan of salvation for mankind. The Bible is about the truth, not necessarily about scientific fact. It is the account of God speaking to us both directly and through historical events.

If we take *everything* in the Bible literally (except for those parts that are supposed to be taken literally), looking for scientific explanations, then we miss the point. The Bible has to be read, interpreted, and understood within the historical and cultural context in which it was written. Without a thorough understanding of this, one can use a particular verse or story of the Bible to back up all kinds of ridiculous claims and make all sorts of absurd and mistaken points that have absolutely nothing to do with the purpose for which those verses were originally written. Personal interpretation is very dangerous!

For example, as I often point out to folks, take the story of Adam and Eve. Do we know with scientific certainty that the names of the first two human beings were in fact Adam and Eve, and that they lived in a garden, took the bad advice of a snake, and ruined their lives and the lives of all who followed after them? The answer is no. And that isn't the point of the story. The point of the story is to relate to us the truth that God did create everything; that he created everything good, including man and woman; that evil did not come from the hand of God; that mankind was made the steward of creation, was given free will so that he may love freely — and as a result of disobeying God, brought sin into the world; and that this first sin, this first act of disobedience, did truly bring chaos, disorder, and evil into the world.

Throughout the Bible, especially in the Old Testament, many stories are used to make a theological statement and to reveal truth. We see this reality in simple secular stories as well. We are all familiar with "The Boy Who Cried Wolf" story. Who cares who the boy was and what kind of wolf it was? Trying to figure out the historical roots and the minuscule scientific details, and seeking to prove the actual, factual existence of the boy and the wolf in the story, would be a ridiculous waste of time (though perhaps still interesting). The point of the story, obviously, is to reveal to us the truth that telling lies and being dishonest will get one into trouble — and big trouble at that!

Jesus also told stories (parables) to relate the truth of a particular matter. But keep in mind that the Bible is not just about fantastic stories. Naturally, the Scriptures are also full of actual historical events of God working in and through certain people, cultures, times, and places in which he thus made his presence known and brought about his revelation and his plan of salvation.

What makes the Old Testament of primary importance is the fact that it contains the prophecies, or the foretelling, of the coming of the Messiah, the Christ, the "anointed one." Jesus, and no one else, fulfilled all of these prophecies. "What were they?" you ask. They were, to name a few (get ready now), that:

- He would be born of a virgin.
- He would be a descendant of Abraham.
- He would come from the tribe of Judah, of the house of David.
- He would be born in Bethlehem, taken to Egypt, and survive Herod's killing of the infants.
- He would be anointed by the Holy Spirit and heralded by a messenger of the Lord (John the Baptist).
- He would perform miracles, preach good news, minister in Galilee, and cleanse the Temple.
- He would present himself as king — 173,880 days from the time of the decree to rebuild Jerusalem — and enter the Holy City as a king on a donkey.
- He would be rejected by the Jews and die a violent, humiliating death that consisted of: rejection and betrayal, being sold for 30 pieces of silver; remaining silent before his accusers; being mocked, beaten, and spat upon; having his hands and feet pierced; being crucified alongside thieves; praying for his persecutors; being given gall and vinegar to drink; not sustaining any broken bones in the midst of his torture; having his side pierced; having his garments become the prize for casting lots; and being buried in a rich man's tomb.
- He would, after all that, rise from the dead, ascend into heaven, and finally be seated at the right hand of the Father.

The probability of one person fulfilling all these prophecies is one in billions upon billions upon billions. But still there are skeptics who say, "Now wait a minute. How do we know all these so-called prophecies were not just predictions that were made up after all the events of Jesus' earthly ministry took place, to then give him credibility?"

The "proof" came about in 1947 with the groundbreaking, earth-shattering discovery of the Dead Sea Scrolls, which are an extensive collection of Jewish Scripture, including texts from almost every book that is in the current Old Testament of the Bible. Miraculously, many of these scrolls were sitting intact (funny how that all works out!) in caves in the northern Dead Sea area of Qumran. Carbon 14 dating, along with paleographic- and scribal-dating methods, verified that most of these scrolls were written somewhere between 335 and 100 B.C. — thus, these messianic prophecies existed loooong before Jesus' time here on earth. Who says science and religion can't work together?

Along with the Dead Sea Scrolls, there are other texts that contained these prophecies before Jesus' time, such as the Septuagint version of the Hebrew Scriptures, which goes back to 250 B.C. There is also prophecy that comes from non-Jewish sources, such as those of the ancient Greeks and Asians, although these are still heavily debated and not yet "proven." But despite the overwhelming scientific and statistical data (which, by the way, come from secular sources), some still doubt. There are even those who claim that Jesus was just a fictional character who existed only on paper and in the minds of believers, that he was not an actual historical person.

Well, here again, despite the Mickey Mouse "research" of truly laughable "scholars" who try so desperately to disprove the existence and authenticity of Christ (most likely out of a guilty conscience), there is an abundance of sources, which historians have confirmed, that tell us otherwise. First, we have the writings of Flavius Josephus, a first-century historian who speaks of Jesus, "the so-called Christ," who was a wise man, performed surprising feats, was crucified under Pilate, and whose followers became known as Christians, etc.

Another source of non-biblical evidence of Jesus and early Christianity can be found in the letters of Pliny the Younger, which were written to Emperor Trajan. Pliny was the Roman governor of Bithynia, in Asia Minor, and in a letter written around A.D. 112, he asks for Trajan's guidance concerning the prudent method to conduct legal proceedings against those accused of being Christians. In a particular section of this letter, Pliny describes with great detail the beliefs and practices of the early followers of Jesus.

Next, one can consider the first-century Roman author Tacitus, who is thought of as the most accurate historian of the ancient world. In his writings, he mentions what he sees as the "superstitious" Christians. He also makes note of the fact that this "Christ" suffered under Pontius Pilate during the reign of Tiberius.

Just to give you a few more examples before we move on, there is the Babylonian Talmud, which hails from the fifth century. This work confirms the crucifixion of Jesus on the eve of the Passover, and it speaks of the accusations leveled against Jesus for "practicing sorcery and encouraging Jewish apostasy." Another source is a second-century Greek writer by the name of Lucian of Samosata, who reveals that Jesus was worshiped by "Christians," that he brought about new teachings, and was put to death on a cross for their sake.

Of course, we also have the writings of the Church Fathers, who were instrumental in handing on the true faith from the apostles of Jesus to the early Christian communities. There are, in addition, such documents as the Gnostic gospels of Thomas, Mary, Judas, and Philip, which were not accepted by Christians then, just as they are not now; but they still, nonetheless, provide historical evidence of Jesus outside the pages of the Bible.

I could go on and on with more information and details here — but if I did, this book would be about 400 pages long before we'd even get to all the hunting and fishing stuff! So, to sum things up a bit, we see that Jesus did exist historically;

that he was preannounced; that he was the fulfillment of many, many detailed prophecies; and that, while the founders and figures of other major religions simply pointed toward God, Jesus claimed to be — and was and is — God. Jesus said that he is "the way, and the truth, and the life," and that there is no other way than through him (Jn 14:6). This states very boldly that the Church, and the faith, that Jesus came to establish is the one true religion. None of this is meant to be a criticism of other religions, but simply a look at the facts.

And so it is in the person of Jesus and in his teachings (the Gospel) that we come to know exactly who God is, what God is like, what he asks and commands of us, what his plan is for us, and so on. In Jesus, the guesswork is taken out, and we no longer have to rely on incomplete or broken "tracks" that merely point us in the right direction. In Jesus Christ, the mystery is solved (somewhat), but faith is still the key component.

Perceiving the Truth

Looking back at all we've covered to this point, one can still simply say, "Yeah, that makes sense and sounds great, but I just don't believe it all. I don't believe in the miracles of Jesus or in the 'miracles' that continue to happen today for that matter. I don't believe in what he taught. I still don't believe that he is God."

We see in Scripture that even one of Jesus' own apostles (Thomas) didn't believe until he saw for himself. Doubt is nothing new, and it plagues us all. It is that which takes away our ability to truly see. But just because we don't believe something or see something doesn't mean it's not there or that it's not true.

Let me give an example. I was born with color blindness. Certain shades of green and gray are mixed up in my perception. But it works to my advantage — "sniper vision" is what they called it, during World War II. Ever since I was a kid, I could hike through the woods with my family or friends and pick out snakes, frogs, lizards, and various other animals that remained virtually invisible to everybody else. Because of my color "blindness," the natural camouflage of those critters didn't work on me. To me, they stood out like that "sore thumb" we always hear about. (By the way, whose thumb is that?) On one hike in particular that I remember, I pointed out a snake to my mother, and she simply did not believe it was there until I poked it with a stick to get it to move. As she then experienced, it *was* there! Her initial doubt and lack of perception did not negate the reality of its existence.

Likewise, our doubt and inability to truly see are what cause us to lose the trail while tracking God, even though it is he who is all the while tracking us! If God revealed himself to us in ways that satisfied our incredible faithlessness, and if Jesus did everything that people wanted him to do in order to "prove" himself (then and now), then all of us would believe, hands down, no questions asked. Thus, we would have no choice but to know, love, and serve God. To even ask a question or even consider having to grapple with "proofs" and "arguments" for God's existence would be utter foolishness. It would be as obvious as looking at a brick wall and saying, "Ah yes, there it is! If I doubt that wall's existence, all I have to do is ram my head into it, crack my thick skull, and knock myself unconscious."

Free Will, Faith, and True Sight

But as we know, this notion of having to prove himself is not how God works, and that's because he has given us freedom. He has given us freedom because he wants us to freely love him as he loves us. As all those old country songs say, we can't *make* somebody love us. It has to be a free choice, a free act of the will.

Thus, God has given us free will. And with it, we may love him or hate him; we may come to know him intimately and lovingly; or we may defiantly reject him. By our free will, we can make ourselves saints or whiskey-bent, hollow-eyed, hell-bound, flesh-mongering, godless, faithless, pagan hedonists. We can bring beauty, wonder, peace, and love into our world, or we can bring ugliness, chaos, bedlam, discord, and an unquenchable hate. The choice is ours: we are free to choose the good, or fail. And in failing, we become slaves to our self-made world of atrocities, selfishness, and greed.

The topic of free will always brings one big question to mind: *If God knows everything that I'm going to do, then am I really free?* Yes, you are. I know that the sun will rise tomorrow morning, but I didn't cause it to come up. I may plant a seed, water it, fertilize it, and know that it will grow, but I am not responsible for the process by which it develops and grows. As Archbishop Fulton Sheen used to point out, it's in a similar manner that God knows the outcome of our actions and decisions, but he does not force us to act or decide as we do. Just as we view the events of something on a time line, one by one, so God sees and comprehends the whole thing at once, like flying over a battlefield and taking it all in instantaneously, instead of watching one fight at a time. He dwells in the eternal now.

Getting back to faith, it is by developing our faith that we come to know the unknown, see the unseen, hear in silence, and experience the reality of God in our lives. It is by faith, reason, and a mountain of tangible data that we come to know Jesus Christ, who is the fulfillment of God's revelation to mankind. The more time we spend with God — listening to his word and observing the wonders of his creation — the more we come to know him in an intimate, very personal manner. Faith gives us the awareness that a master tracker has for what he seeks. We come to simply know what it is we seek, that it is there, and that to deny the track would be the height of absurdity and denial. The more we use our spiritual tracking ability, and the more we develop it and exercise it, the stronger it gets, until we don't need to exercise it at all: it simply is. And that which simply is, is God.

So open the eyes of your soul, and learn to truly see! But right now, let's get to the hunt. Read on!

Chapter 2

TURKEY LOVE

KABOOM!!! AND WITH THAT, the recoil from the 3½-inch magnum, 12-gauge turkey load hit me in the shoulder like a devastating knockout blow from a rage-filled Mike Tyson in his prime! When the reverberations from the shock wore off, and I could see straight and clear again, I moseyed downrange 40 yards to where my turkey-head target was placed. I knelt down in the soft fragrant dirt and meticulously counted the number of pellet holes that were in the vitals. As you well-seasoned hunters know, at least 3 pellets are needed to make a killing shot on a turkey, so when my count reached 17, I was more than happy.

A confident, satisfied smile eased across my face as I boldly stood up, took a deep breath of pollen-filled air into my lungs, raised my unshaven chin, looked to the hills, raised my trusty shotgun over my head and hollered, "I've got you now, dirty birdy!" (All in good fun, of course.) I loaded up a few more rounds, did a little more target practice for good measure, and then cleaned my foreboding weapon and put it back in the cumbersome plastic case, where it would anxiously, yet patiently, rest until its impressive might would be summoned the following week.

As I loaded up my gear and drove back home, I couldn't help but reflect on all the humiliating mishaps and disasters that have taken place over the last decade or so of turkey hunting. If you read *Hunting for God, Fishing for the Lord*, then you're well aware of all the bad luck and misfortune that have come my way while pursuing the majestic Eastern gobbler. It just could not get any worse. I've experienced the most terrible things imaginable that the world of the wild turkey could dish out, including a death-defying flash flood and almost being shot by a sneaking, idiotic trespasser. Although I'd polished my hunting, scouting, and calling abilities to the level of a skilled, experienced hunter, I still had nothing to show for it. Something would always — and I mean *always* — go wrong at the last second.

Season after season, I was able to locate, set up on, and call gobblers right in like clockwork. But every time, the birds would either "hang up" (hesitate to come closer), come in behind me, stay behind an obstacle, get run off by coyotes or wild dogs, or something else. I simply could not close the deal! I was convinced beyond the shadow of a doubt that I had some kind of turkey-hunting hex on me. I just couldn't win, no matter what. I began to feel that it was of no use to even hope for a filled turkey tag.

Despite all the bad luck and disastrous mishaps, though, as I'm always quick to point out, I never really get too upset about it. I just love being out there. I love talking with the birds and hearing them let loose that thunderous, spine-tingling, electrifying gobble. There are truly few things on earth like it! To be out in the woods on a glorious, cool spring morning — and to watch the sun come up and to be an intimate spectator and participant in nature's rite of spring — is a tremendous gift and privilege. It's just impossible for me to go home mad after spending a day in such an exhilarating, awe-inspiring atmosphere.

And so at last, the opening morning of the 2007 season arrived. My turkey-hunting vest, and all my gear, was organized with great German efficiency as usual. Everything was in its place and ready to go. As I drove the last mile to the farm, I offered a prayer of thanksgiving to the Lord, as I always do, for the opportunity and honor to be enjoying his marvelous creation once again, and I asked his blessings upon the landowners who so graciously let me spend time on their property.

To finish off my pre-hunt meditation, I spent some time reminiscing with the Almighty about all the good times we'd had in the woods together, and I said: "Lord, you're always my best hunting partner; there is no one I'd rather hunt with than you. Be with me today. Let my first bird be one that just you and I harvest together." And with that, I arrived and parked my truck.

Still under the cover of darkness, I slowly stalked through the woods and did some locator calls to try and get a gobbler to sound off in the brisk April air. No luck. Not a peep! I decided to set up once again on my favorite ridge top, to await the sunrise and listen to where the birds were, since I had not been able to pinpoint their location the evening prior.

I nestled into the tangled, twisted remains of a recently fallen tree and prepared my calls and my decoy setup. When everything was ready to go, I melted into the stoic, silent stillness. Within a few minutes, the tapestry of glorious nothingness was interrupted as I heard soft approaching footsteps — a deer, no doubt. A little later, I heard the first movement of an early morning songbird symphony. The air was filled with melodically joyful chirps and whistles — a lovely prelude indeed!

As the predawn gloom evolved into a hint of beer-like amber glow of sunlight, the sweet sounds intensified. Suddenly, a voice rose above the rest like the sharp staccato of an emerging trumpet solo; a crow squawked with sharp, aggressive vigor. The counterpoint to this sonic statement was what I'd been waiting to hear all year: "Gooobleloobleeeee!" Although the bird was far away, that was my cue from the Divine Conductor. I raised my slate call and performed a few gentle, sleepy, coaxing notes, "Yelp . . . yelp . . . yelp," as if to say in turkey talk: "Oh be quiet. I'm still here, you jealous fool! Now go back to sleep."

As the primetime of sunrise continued, and as I did my best to gently elicit some passionate gobbling, I heard very little. And the few gobbles that I did hear were way off in the distance. My heart began to sink. This was far below my expectations for an opening morning in the turkey woods. I couldn't remember the last time that I'd heard so few gobbles on the first day of the season, with the exception of bad weather as a factor.

Perhaps the predictions were true: maybe this would be a very difficult season. It was reported in March that Missouri had experienced the warmest weather in 118 years, which apparently influenced the turkeys to start breeding — but then, in early April, the temperatures plummeted. A winter-like freeze swept across the land, killing crops, causing foliage damage, and inducing the birds to abandon their nests and go back to their cold-weather flock behavior.

Still reeling from disappointment, but all the while enthusiastic nonetheless, I decided to creep down into the valley to see if perhaps any birds were sneaking around in the bottoms. At around 7:35, I set up in the cover of another fallen tree and set my decoys out about 15 yards in front of me. I waited a few minutes and then did a series of calling, "Yelp ... yelp ... yelp ... Purrrrr ... purrrrr. . . . Yelp ... YELP. . . . Cut! Cut! Cut! CUT!" Off to my left, I heard the still distant but immediate response of Mr. Tom Turkey singing solo: "Gobble ... gobbleeee!"

Ah yes! There were a few birds down there ... as usual. I waited about 15 minutes and repeated my desperate plea for affection: "Cut-cut! Purrrr-cut! Yelp ... yelp. . . . Purrr-cut! Cut! Cut! Cut!" Right in the middle of that final sequence, I was pleasingly startled as a loud, raspy gobble shot right back at me from within the thick cedars just across the way. He was right on top of me — but where exactly?

Just seconds after I heard that gobble, I saw a bobbing red, white, and blue head sneaking along the fence line 40 yards to my left, back in the brush. I didn't have much of a shot because of all the obstructions, so I had to wait and see if he'd move into a more open area. The bird began to cluck with a tone of great excitement, but he seemed to be getting aggravated. He was darting back and forth along the barbed-wire fence looking for a place to get through and come my way.

Unexpectedly, he disappeared into the thick woods, and his clucking began to slowly fade away. *Oh no! He got so frustrated that he left*, I thought to myself. Shortly after that notion slipped out of my dense skull and evaporated into the humid air, the clucking began getting louder — and it was coming from directly behind me. Since I was sitting against a large fallen tree, I was able to crouch down, get turned around, and carefully get into a perfect position to make a shot without the bird spotting me.

As the moment of truth was at hand, I suddenly began to hear a loud thumping sound, as if an elephant were rampaging through the woods in search of a harassing native to stomp into the dirt like a measly ant. *Wait a minute*, I realized. *That sound is my heart thumping!* Along with my pounding chest, my breathing grew rapid and deep, as if I were on the verge of hyperventilating. Realizing my imminent unraveling, I began to coach myself: *Calm down ... calm down, Joey ol' boy. Relax ... take your time ... settle down.* I quickly got control of myself and settled in for the shot.

Three crafty Missouri longbeards

Down the hill and through the woods the turkey came, until he finally showed himself. He was a good-sized bird, although the short beard protruding from his chest let me know he was a "jake" (a juvenile gobbler), but still a legal bird to take. When his eyes locked onto my decoys, he got even more excited and let out another gobble, while exploding into a full-strut position to show off his wears to "the ladies." When he stopped strutting, his feathers deflated back to normal. As he moved in a few more steps, I took a deep breath, let half of it out, and waited for him to move just a little to the right where I had a perfectly clear opening to shoot.

Just as I was about to let loose with that long-awaited shot, the big black bird started nervously scampering around, as if he knew something wasn't right. His clucking began to sound more like a "putt," an alarm that turkeys make before they bolt out of an area. I did a few very soft "purrs" to calm him down, and in response he finally took that final step into position. My concentration and focus were steady and unbreakable. My nerves and eyes were harnessed into a steely death ray, like a tiger about to pounce on his prey. I quickly but carefully lined up the sighting beads on my shotgun and squeeeeezzzzzed the trigger.

Kaboom!!! This time the shoulder-dislocating recoil of my turkey gun didn't even faze me. The bird's head jolted back in a cloud of gunpowder and feathers, as he instantly fell to the forest floor like a sack of potatoes. I watched for a few seconds to make sure he was fully expired and then let out the other half of that deep, pre-shot breath: "Phhhssseeeeewwwoooooaaa."

With all that internal pressure released, I emptied my gun and walked 35 steps or so to where my bird lay beside a well-aged, moss-covered log. I double-checked that he did, in fact, have a beard and spurs to make sure he was a legal male bird and that my mind wasn't playing tricks on me. Sure enough, I had just harvested my first turkey. It wasn't the biggest gobbler in the woods, but at 16 1/2 pounds, it was certainly not the skinniest, either. He was quite large and rather mature for a jake.

I picked up the deceased bird and gently placed him on top of the nearby log as if it were a funeral pyre. I sat down next to him and respectfully marveled at the beauty of this creature and thanked the Lord. As I admired the sleek, almost reflective, black, brown, bronze, and golden hues of the turkey's magnificent plumage, a feeling of calmness came over me. I examined his pointy beak, huge wings, and that trademark tail fan.

The woods were still. Even though it was only a little before 8 a.m., it felt as though I'd been out there all day. As the sun was still on its ascent, beams of light cascaded down through the leafy canopy overhead like the smoke of blessed incense expanding and filling a great cathedral of Europe. Fresh dew glistened on the emerging greenery all around me. I sat there for several minutes in the sacred silence, with a heart now bursting, not with adrenaline, but with gratitude.

Father Joe and the makings of several turkey dinners

At last I proudly picked up the bird again, slung him over my shoulder (with my orange safety flag hanging out of my vest), and slowly, but joyfully, stepped "truckward." Upon getting back to my trusty vehicle, I set up my camera for a few shots, shared the story with the landowners, and then started burning up the phone lines as I retold the story and shared the excitement with all my hunting buddies. What a marvelous day it was! The turkey-hunting hex was over! The curse had been broken! I would finally partake in a wild turkey feast in which I (and the Lord) provided the bird. I was on cloud nine to say the least!

When the initial excitement of that day finally wore off and had transformed into yet another cherished memory that will forever be etched in the annals of my heart and soul, I found myself once again reflecting about the hunt on a deeper, more poignant level.

Besides the fact that I just enjoy being in the woods so much, there are three reasons I didn't throw in the towel on turkey hunting long ago and just move on to something else to do in the spring: faith, hope, and love.

The Power of Faith, Hope, and Love

In the turkey seasons that followed, I filled most of my tags lickety-split. I even harvested my first bow-and-arrow turkey, which is an exceptionally difficult feat. Having hunted for well over a decade with no luck, no turkey tags filled, and countless heartaches and disappointments would seemingly have been more than enough reason for any sane individual to simply sell his shotgun and buy some golf clubs. (Never!) But I didn't give up. It was faith, hope, and love that kept me going and instilled a patient perseverance, through all those years of woodland misery and humiliating failed attempts, to close the deal with Mr. Tom Turkey.

I briefly discussed faith in the previous chapter, but generically, we can define *faith* as the knowledge, trust, confidence, and belief in something or someone that is not "proven." I never gave up turkey hunting because I did, in fact, have an absolute trust, complete confidence, and undying belief that despite the seemingly impossible odds, I would be successful. I believed that sooner or later (never realizing it would be much, much later) I would break the turkey-hunting curse.

I didn't know why it was taking so long, and I didn't have any rational explanation for this conspicuously orchestrated string of bad luck, but it was faith that fueled the fire to carry on. I believe now that it was part of God's plan. All that bad luck, and all those trials and tribulations, produced three chapters worth of material for books and also sparked several friendships with other turkey hunters around the country. Once again, God allowed (not caused) all the bad stuff to happen so that good could come from it.

While *faith* is the knowledge of, and trust in, something or someone when there is no "proof," *hope* can be defined as a feeling of confidence. It is a feeling that things will work out in a positive manner. Keep in mind that it is possible, at times, to have faith in something but not always to have hope. For example, I have *faith* that someday God will call me home, that I will die, but I certainly do not *hope* for it anytime soon!

Over all those years of turkey-less turkey hunting, I never lost hope. I knew, and had faith, that I would one day be successful — but I also had an untarnishable hope. Although I'll admit it was hard sometimes to muster, and difficult to hold on to, I still always possessed a feeling that any day could be *the* day. Despite the (at times) overwhelming negativity, there was constantly present the bright light of hope deep down within that kept me going.

Finally, it was because of love that I refused to burn my turkey tags and sell all my gear on eBay out of defeat and dismal failure. Now, "love" is a very strong word that should not be used lightly. I've discussed this in *Hunting for God, Fishing for the Lord*, so I won't repeat it all again here. But "love" is not a word to throw around casually, even though we all (including me) do. I *love* a good peanut butter sandwich. There are, however, different kinds of love that have different implications and deserve thorough explanations, which I addressed in my second book, *Meat & Potatoes Catholicism*. But, generally speaking, we can define *love* as an intense, passionate, affectionate attraction that fosters self-sacrifice and commitment. It's not just a matter of really, really, really liking something or someone, as we so often allude to in our casual use of the word.

That being said, I can honestly say that I truly love turkey hunting, and all forms of outdoor activity. I love it! I'm passionate about it. I have an intense attraction to it. I make many, many sacrifices for it. And I'm firmly committed to it. But, of course, this love is not just about filling tags, putting meat in the freezer, and being immersed in the natural world. At the root of it all, the absolute object of this love is God. It's through being in his magnificent creation, through respectfully harvesting his creation to sustain my life (as God intended), and sharing those experiences with family and friends that I come into contact and union with God. I genuinely love the great outdoors because it's a catalyst to enter more deeply into the greatest love of all: the love of God.

The Nature of Virtue

In Catholic theology, we call faith, hope, and love "theological virtues." I realize that many of you reading this book are not Catholic, but don't worry: these things apply to all. Before we look at these three virtues and how they help form a rock-solid, impenetrable foundation for one's life, it's good to first understand what exactly a virtue is. By definition, a *virtue* is a habit of goodness. Virtue is the strong disposition to do good, to be good, and to be a vehicle and catalyst to bring about more goodness.

To simply sum it up — although I hate this phrase — *virtue* is "to be a good person." The reason I hate this phrase, and the philosophy of just "being a good person," so much is that it's so often used as a cop-out. I've known people who have been involved in all sorts of horrible, unmentionable evils, yet they justify it by saying, "I'm still a good person!" The truth is, we are all good people. We were created by a good God for goodness, but good people do bad things. Good people do terrible things. Good people do truly evil things.

So, then, the questions that come into play in defining virtue are: What does it mean to be genuinely good? Is "being good" just a matter of saying something nice or doing something pleasant for somebody every now and then? Is being "good" not letting foul, filthy, quick-tempered, hot-headed, four-letter expletives fly out of one's mouth, in fear of it being washed out with soap by one's mother? Is being "good" simply going through life in an unassuming, non-aggressive, passive manner, never stepping on someone's toes? No, no, and no are the answers.

As many great theological minds have pointed out over the years, a thing is "good" if it fulfills the purpose for which it was made. For example, the keyboard on which I'm typing these words is "good" so long as it produces the letters and performs the functions for which it was designed. If I hit the "A" key and a "Z" shows up, or if I hit a key and it sticks or breaks, it is not a "good" keyboard; it would, in fact, be a "bad" keyboard because it is not fulfilling its purpose for existing and for which it was designed and manufactured.

Another example of something being "bad" would be if I tried to use my keyboard as a fish-filleting board. Sure, it has a nice rectangular shape and is set at the proper angle to fillet a fish upon; but as the fish scales and malodorous, slimy gunk would seep into the spaces between the keys, it would no doubt end up as a big disgusting mess! Thus, my keyboard would make a very "bad" fillet board because it is trying to be used for something it was not made and designed for. This same phenomenon that applies to good and bad things also applies to us as human beings.

Life, Love, and Truth

A person is *good* if he or she attains the purpose for which he or she was made. "And so, what is that purpose?" you ask. Divine revelation teaches us that we were made for life, love, and truth, and it's only in attaining these things that we become genuinely, perfectly happy. Furthermore, the only absolute source of life, truth, and love is God. The only "bad" news is that we cannot attain the complete and total fullness of these things while on earth; we can only do so in heaven.

We can try as hard as we can to sustain life, to bring life about and defend it, but in the end we lose it — it is still ravaged by age and disease, and it is snuffed out by violence. We can fill our minds with vast amounts of knowledge and objective scientific facts as we search for the truth, but the search will never end, and total knowledge cannot be fully achieved; there is always more to know, and there are mysteries that will never be explained, which are far beyond our human ability to reason and comprehend. And as much as we may experience the sweetness and completion that love brings into our lives, that, too, will fade and come to an end here on earth.

The reason we cannot experience the fullness of life, truth, and love in our lives here on earth is because of evil, which mankind is responsible for bringing into the world through disobedience and sin. When we sin, we break the moral law that governs the universe as designed and revealed by God. Whether we admit it or not, and no matter how hard we may try to block out the guilt of sin in our lives, we all know when we have committed it: our conscience, that voice within us, tells us we have done right or wrong.

For many, though, their conscience is rendered virtually useless because it is not properly informed, reformed, and conformed. For others, their conscience is silenced by the constant subliminal rejection of it. When this is the case, the gravity and reality of sin is greatly disguised, and thus the guilt that comes from sin comes out in other ways, such as depression, addiction, atheism, pessimism, and a multitude of negative behaviors and attitudes. This is because, deep down, we know when we have revolted against the moral law that God has placed within us. And doing so is a punishment in and of itself, because it makes our lives miserable.

God gave us a moral law, and he commands us to be obedient to it because he knows good and well what will happen to us if we are not: we will lose the peace and joy that he has given us, the peace and joy he wants us to experience in life. But, still, the choice is ours, and God respects our freedom.

Virtue and morality, which we're essentially talking about here, are based on the ability to choose what is good and reject what is evil — and this ability defines true freedom. As I've already mentioned, we have the freedom to make ourselves into something great by choosing that which is good, or into something terrible by rejecting the good and being mastered and enslaved by sin. Greatness comes by choosing that which leads to life, truth, and love — and, very importantly, by making that choice out of love for the one (God) who has given us these things, not out of fear of punishment or consequence.

Another word for this greatness is "holiness." To be *holy* means to live a life rooted in, and connected to, the life, truth, and love that have their purpose and fulfillment in God. To be "unholy," then, means to be evil. There is, however, a big difference between being bad and being evil. Doing something *bad* means to make a mistake; doing something *evil* means to seek to purposely destroy (to varying degrees) that which is good.

Going back to my keyboard as an example, for me to use it as a filleting board would be bad; it would be a mistake to try to use it for a purpose for which it was not designed. For me to use my keyboard as a head-smashing club to attack and kill someone would not only be bad (a mistaken use), but it would also be downright evil, in that I'm purposely using it to destroy that which is good.

Principal Virtues

To boil things down and clarify things a bit more, the top priority for you and me is to do that which is truly "good" and avoid that which is "bad" — and more importantly, to avoid at all costs that which is evil. Going back to square one, virtue is how we do that. *Virtue* is developing a habit of doing good and of striving for life, truth, and love — all of which is striving for God, in all we do. There are four primary, or principal, virtues that help us do this. We call them "cardinal virtues," and they are *prudence, fortitude, justice,* and *temperance.*

Prudence is having the practical wisdom to know what to do and say in certain situations, and what *not* to do and say in other situations. It's knowing when to make a bold, or not-so-bold, move in defense of what is "good," and when to do the same to avoid evil. *Fortitude* is the internal strength to actually carry out that plan of action with courage and integrity. *Justice* is to seek what is right and fair, and to ensure that every individual is treated righteously and fairly. *Temperance,* finally, is the virtue that helps us resist those things that entice us into doing evil. It is that which helps us reject temptation and to consciously avoid the near occasions of sin, because, again, sin only makes us miserable in the end.

The practice of these four principal virtues helps us to avoid the opposite of virtue, which is vice. A *vice* is a habit of sin and evil. It steals away our freedom and makes us slaves. It's important to realize, though, that many times our vices may be centered on things that are in and of themselves good.

One of the ways we can sin is by choosing something that is initially good, but attaining it or using it in a way that is not good — that is, in a disordered way. Here are two examples:

- Food is good. But too much of it, too little of it, or the uncontrollable desire to consume it is not good.
- Sexual activity (in the proper context of committed, married love between a man and a woman) is good. Sexual

activity outside of that context is not good; it brings about disease, death, dehumanization, emotional trauma, unwanted pregnancies, the destruction of unborn children, and on and on.

Thus, things that are good — things that are gifts from God, to experience his goodness of life, truth, and love — can become things that we use in a disordered (bad) way. They can become vices, which will in the end — you guessed it — make us and our world miserable!

Just as the four cardinal virtues described here are the foundation that our lives as human beings are built upon, so the "theological virtues" of *faith*, *hope*, and *love* are the foundation for our lives as Christians. Although I've discussed these three virtues earlier in a rather generic fashion, and reflected on how they helped my outdoor endeavors, they have much deeper implications for us as men and women of God.

Faith, spiritually defined by the *Catechism of the Catholic Church*, is "the theological virtue by which we believe in God and believe all that he has said and revealed to us, and that Holy Church [through Sacred Scripture and Sacred Tradition] proposes for our belief, because he is truth itself"; by means of faith, we freely commit ourselves to know God and to do his will (CCC 1814). Faith, in this sense, is not just about knowing and believing but also a commitment to live in accordance with that knowledge and belief in God.

As followers of Christ, we are called not just to have, keep, profess, and be witnesses to our faith, but also to nourish it and, most importantly, to fervently practice it, despite opposition and persecution. If we don't practice our faith in our daily lives, we deny it — and Christ — by our omission. We do not necessarily "earn" our way into heaven; but if we say one thing and yet do another, we contradict the faith we claim to be "saved" by. It's from this premise that, as St. James teaches, *faith without works is dead* (see Jas 2:17).

It's because of our faith that we then have hope. *Hope* is "the theological virtue by which we desire the kingdom of heaven and eternal life as our happiness, placing our trust in Christ's promises and relying not on our own strength, but on the help of the grace of the Holy Spirit" (CCC 1817). It is hope that keeps us optimistic and joyful throughout the many hardships we endure in life. Our hope in the Lord and in eternal life is that which purifies our lives, keeps us focused on virtue, and motivates us to avoid sinfulness and vice.

It's this hope, fueled by faith, that instills our hearts with love. *Love*, as a theological virtue, is often referred to as "charity." This love, or charity, is that "by which we love God above all things for his own sake, and our neighbor as ourselves for the love of God" (CCC 1822). However, charity, or love, is not just something we strive for, but something we are commanded to do. In John's Gospel, we hear Jesus say:

> "This is my commandment, that you love one another as I have loved you. Greater love has no man than this, that a man lay down his life for his friends. You are my friends if you do what I command you." (Jn 15:12-14)

So again, real love is a self-sacrificing love that is focused on the good of the other (and don't forget what "good" entails). As St. Paul so beautifully said:

> Love is patient and kind; love is not jealous or boast-ful; it is not arrogant or rude. Love does not insist on its own way; it is not irritable or resentful; it does not rejoice at wrong, but rejoices in the right. Love bears all things, believes all things, hopes all things, endures all things. (1 Cor 13:4-7)

The next line of that passage is exceptionally powerful: *Love never fails!* We may fail at many things in life, whether it is in a relationship, at having the courage to do the right thing, at avoiding evil, or at something as simple as a turkey hunt. But it is the love of God, the truth of God, and the life he gives us that keep us going. Love will never fail to give us hope and to strengthen our faith. Love will never fail to help us form a habit of virtue and to stay free from the slavery of vice. Love will never fail to motivate us to succeed. This is the true meaning of the biblical passage "God is love" (1 Jn 4:8).

Indeed he is. Amen!

Chapter 3

HOG WILD!

FROM THE DAY my pearly white teeth (now yellow from coffee) were strong enough to chomp and chew on a savory pork steak, and my tongue conditioned enough to withstand the slight burn of spicy barbecue sauce, I've had a great love for pig meat! Oh boy! Ribs, ham, steaks, tenderloin, sausage, roasts, sandwiches — whatever pork could be made into, and however it could be served, I liked it! Not to mention how I enjoy those delicious fried pork rinds!

The "other white meat" is one of America's favorite and most popular foods. And as I often say, one of the ways God's sense of humor comes through is in the fact that the dirtiest, filthiest, and most stinking and ugliest critters on land or sea are the tastiest!

Like most everyone else, I suspect, all I knew about pigs as a kid was that they were rather pinkish in color, big and fat; that they stunk like heck; that they had beady little eyes, a curlicued tail, flappy ears, a very unique-looking nose; and that they had a vocabulary that consisted of assorted oinks, snorts, squeals, and grunts. I never had any interest in hunting one, or even knew they could be hunted, for that matter, until I was in the fifth grade. Until then, I just thought all pigs dwelled on farms and lived out their existence in muddy pens, with big feeding troughs to stuff their fat, piggy faces in — morning, noon, and night.

All that changed one day when, as a youngster, I walked into what was a new local archery shop and saw the mounted head of the most hideous, scariest, wildest-looking beast I'd ever seen hanging on the wall! It was none other the wild boar, complete with coarse black hair, a long demon-like tongue, pro-truding razor-sharp tusks, and a thick mane on the back of its head and neck. The piercing stare from those hate-filled, fear-some glass eyes filled me with terror! I remember thinking if that thing were alive and got hold of me, he'd throw me around like a rag doll, chew me up like a piece of stale beef jerky, and kick me into the abrasive dirt like a grubby worm.

"I would hate to ever meet up with one of those," I said to the man behind the counter, as I gazed in awe at the abominable creature.

Noticing my youthful curiosity, the archery-shop guy told me all about the exciting hunt for that particular pig, and he also gave me a little education concerning the wild boar. I found out that the wild pigs which are roaming North America these days come from one of three sources: they are descendants from the original strain of hogs brought here from Europe in the 1500s; they are feral hogs (domestic pigs that have escaped from captivity and gone wild again); they are a combination of the two.

Wild pigs, much like any other wild animal, like to live in areas of wilderness where there is abundant food and water. Boars (and sows for that matter) can run as fast as lightning and also are able to swim with the best of them! Pigs do not have sweat glands (so much for "sweating like a pig"), so they have to roll around in mud and slop (which often contains their own waste) to stay cool — hence their dirty, stinking, malodorous reputation.

Wild hogs eat all kinds of things. They have the appetite of, well, a fat greedy pig! They are omnivores, like you and me, so they have a diet that can consist of a great variety of food. They'll eat acorns and other nuts, fruit, roots, grass, insects, birds, other animals (alive or dead), mushrooms, eggs, and other such edible delights.

Pigs, wild or domestic, are not the clumsy, dumb oafs they may appear to be. On the contrary, they are one of the most nimble and intelligent animals around — and when living in the wild, they develop and rely on that intelligence all the more. A wild pig has an incredible sense of smell, just like that of the ever-wary whitetail deer. Although a boar's eyesight is not all that good, it can keenly detect movement and thereby elude the few threats it faces in the wild — man being the greatest.

The hog also has an acute sense of hearing; and while the domestic pig's ears lazily flop over, the wild boar's are always straight up, on full alert. To top it all off, a wild boar has what's called a "shield," which is a thick layer of hardened fat around his neck and shoulders that functions like armor plating. The bigger and older a boar gets, and the more fighting it does, the thicker and tougher the plate gets, making it all the more challenging for a rival to be victorious in battle, or for a hunter to administer a killing shot. Adding to the difficulty of bringing down a mighty swine is the fact that its vitals (heart and lungs) are tucked in tight behind its front legs/shoulders and covered by that thick, dense plate.

Add all this up, and you've got a big, tough, fast, smart animal that is built to survive. And if anything gets in the way of that survival, it had better run! While usually rather reclusive, skittish, and secretive, the wild boar is also well known for having a very aggressive, bloodthirsty temperament. Wild boars will attack and fight amongst themselves, with other animals, or with man. A hot-headed hog will think nothing of (and will thoroughly enjoy) ripping apart and killing anything, or anyone, that gets in its way.

It's important to point out, too, that wild pigs are unwanted, unwelcome guests in most states. Because they are not originally native, wild swine that move into an area, or domestic hogs that become feral, will ravage the land, as they tear up roots and kill native plants. Some of them carry all kinds of awful diseases. They cause erosion of lakes, ponds, streams, and rivers by their constant wallowing around, which also can decimate certain fish populations. Boars can wipe out smaller animals, including a variety of endangered species. They are known for wreaking havoc on crops and gardens, not to mention the fact that they eat up all the food which deer, turkeys, and other native animals depend upon. Few inhabitants in the woods are likely to take on and kill a tank-like wild boar, which, by the way, can grow to well over 600 pounds, with some reports of monster hogs over a thousand pounds! Thus, they are hunted to stop their massive ecological destruction.

But it's not just for damage control or "sport" that wild pigs are sought. As the man in the archery shop concluded the day I first set eyes on that magnificent beast of the forest: "You'll never find pork in the store as tasty and lean as from a wild boar." And from my experience, he was certainly right about that! Yum! I do, however, hear that the obscenely huge "Hogzilla-sized" pigs (400-1,000 pounds) are not very good for table fare and are only edible if made into sausage. And who wants to eat (or can eat) a pork steak the size of a car door!

The raging countenance of the wild boar

With my young mind filled with all this pig-knowledge and the image of that defiant, grotesque, yet beautiful, creature forever burned into my brain, I became helplessly fascinated with the wild boar from that day on. Although I've been involved with archery since I was a kid, I didn't start hunting with a bow until my early 20s. But from then until now, I've had an incendiary desire to go one-on-one with the wild boar, the "poor man's grizzly," and harvest some tasty, succulent pork with my archery gear.

A few years ago, I did harvest a wild boar with my trusty rifle. And although it was a very challenging, nerve-racking hunt to say the least — and yes, that pig was just as delicious and nutritious as I could have hoped for — I still look forward to my first wild-boar bow hunt. For me, hunting with a rifle, while I immensely enjoy it, is rather anticlimactic at times. Bowhunting is far more challenging and is much more up close and personal. With a bow and arrow, the hunter more intimately enters into the reality of what is genuinely happening and becomes more in tune with the responsibility of taking life to sustain life. He is also more keenly aware of the importance of doing so in a manner that is fast, clean, and humane.

There is just some instinct inside me that will only be satisfied upon successfully harvesting a huge, wild beast of a boar in one of the most primitive manners possible; with a "stick and a string." Now, when I say "wild" boar, I'm not talking about trapped or farm-raised transplants that commercial "wild boar hunting" operations advertise and stock their ranches with. I'm talking about genuinely wild, killing-machine pigs, the kind that I have a strange desire to wrestle to the ground and roast over an open fire for all to feast upon, under the sullen, pearly hue of a full moon, while ravenous wolves howl their approval from the distant mountaintops!

Why this strange fascination? I can't explain it. Perhaps it's some kind of caveman instinct coming through, inspiring me to perform this great act of self-sufficiency and to feed one's kin by staring death in the face and taking it on with just a pointy stick. Then again, maybe I'm just a crazy idiot! (No nasty comments now, please.)

Hog-Hunting Foolishness

Something that I continue to do as I plan and look forward to my first archery hog hunt is to watch videos and DVDs of wild boar bowhunting. I've been able to pick up lots of good tips and strategies, and I've collected a fair amount of valuable information from watching the "pros of pigs" in action. While most of the videos I've seen are produced by professionals from reputable organizations, there is one that I acquired (through the Internet) which is perhaps the most ridiculous thing I have ever seen in my life! It is a true embarrassment to the hunting community — and to the whole human race for that matter! Out of kindness, and concern of macabre promotion, I won't give you the name of the video, or the real name of the gentlemen who starred in this epic film of foolishness. (Actually, as I recall now, I think I threw it away out of utter disgust.)

Anyhow, the film began with an interview of the mighty hunter, and it went something like this (I am exaggerating here, but not much): "Hello, I'm Bill E. Boarman [not his real name, obviously], and I'm quite possibly the greatest bowhunter that has ever lived. There is simply nobody better than me, and you should be aware of that right now. I've taken some of the biggest wild boars on the face of the earth. I'm the bravest, toughest, most cunning hunter in the land. In this video, you will see just how magnificent my skills are. You will be duly impressed by my astonishing knowledge of boar biology and my incredible ability to spot and stalk these vicious wild creatures. So without further delay, come celebrate my greatness with me and glory in my self-praise!" And with this over-the-top, conceited, arrogant, unbelievably egotistical, self-glorifying rant, the video began.

The opening scene was of Bill E. Boarman giving a brief seminar about wild pig habitat, behavior, and proper arrow placement in order to quickly dispatch a hog. After referring to an anatomical drawing of the wild boar (which looked like something a third-grader drew with a few crayons) and pointing out the kill zone, Bill gave a demonstration of his shooting skills. He set up at 25 yards and shot 3 or 4 arrows with a shaky, quick, feverish pace. Upon examining the outcome, his arrows were in a group, but all over the place on the target, certainly not the kind of pinpoint, arrow-splitting accuracy that a pro, or even an intermediate archer, would display. As Bill looked over the results, he gave a knowing look in the camera and concluded, "Yep, that'll do it! Some of these shots are a bit off, but it'll work."

It was quite obvious that ol' Bill was not the "expert" he claimed to be, and I began to wonder if this video was meant as a joke! After getting some target practice, Bill headed to the hills in search of his quarry.

The next scene began with Bill sweating profusely, huffing and puffing, trying to desperately catch his breath as his enormous gut heaved up and down with each labored gasp for air. As his strained, exhausted words began to form sentences, Bill communicated that he spotted a massive hog down the other side of a deep valley, and that he was hot on its trail. He motioned to the cameraman to follow him and then proceeded to take up the trail once again.

The alarming sounds of fresh twigs snapping, old dense logs crumbling, and crisp leaves crunching filled the hog-stink air with each absurdly loud footstep Bill took as he displayed his "incredibly stealthy stalking skills." His rotund arms and legs swung almost maniacally back and forth like the pendulum of a grand old clock, as he made his way through the pig woods. The amount of noise and commotion he was making would have scared off even a hungry, man-eating grizzly bear. With every passing minute, Mr. Boarman's prideful opening banter was becoming all the more a source of pathetic mockery and side-busting laughter for any viewer who had a lick of sense.

The next scene picked up with our boy finally closing in on his prey. The camera zoomed in on Bill's wide-eyed expression as he nodded in the direction of a huge hairy object in the out-of-focus background. As the view from the fumbling camera began to create a sharper image, a large reddish-brown and black pig came into focus. Noticing the lack of movement from the bedded boar, the cameraman asked inquisitively, "Is it dead?" Bill took a closer look through his high-powered binoculars and reported, "No, he's not dead. He is just asleep."

Needless to say, this wasn't what I had in mind when purchasing an "action-packed, wild-boar hunting, adventure video"! (I've always been a sucker for a flashy cover and slick advertising.) Spotting, stalking, and hunting a ferocious sleeping pig is about the silliest thing I've ever heard of, much less watched. And so, while Mr. Piggy P. Pig slumbered peacefully next to a large brush pile of fallen trees, Bill and his cameraman moved in for the kill. Once again, their breathing became labored with exertion, and now also with the adrenaline-pumped, pre-shot excitement. When he was about 35 yards away, the camera captured Bill heroically drawing back his bow for the narcoleptic "moment of truth."

"Woooooshh . . . Thud . . . SNAP!" . . . went the arrow, as it whizzed over the pig's back, hit a log, and snapped in half. You guessed it — the big hog immediately jolted out of its deep sleep, jumped to its feet, and almost instantly, instinctively, zeroed in on the direction from which the danger came. Then it started. The massive wild beast bristled up his thick mane and began popping its tusks — a sign that you're in big trouble! With the camera still rolling, the microphone picked up the painfully obvious, unscripted dialogue: "Oh no! He's going to charge! G-G-G-Get out your gun, Billy!" Bill answered back, something like, "I can't believe I missed! The Super-Deluxe Pig-Stain

2000 arrow sight on my bow must be off! And I don't have my gun!" As the boar let out a deafening, rage-filled "BBaaaGGR-RRRRrrrrr," he did, in fact, charge the two men. As the determined pig now moved in for its "moment of truth," Bill got off another shot with his bow, this time grazing the top of its head.

It all happened very fast, but it appeared that the seemingly dull arrow jumped off the ramp-like shape of the boar's skull without doing a bit of damage, but it was enough to get the angry pig to turn and run in the other direction. Bill was obviously relieved, and he went back to camp to prepare for round two. As the video progressed, it was just one pathetic display after the next, yet still, the mighty hunter continued his prideful ranting. He had an excuse for everything and tried to make every ignorant blunder look like a feat of true hunting prowess and greatness. I just could not believe it! It was without a doubt one of the most incredible demonstrations of prideful foolishness and vanity I have ever, ever seen!

Good Pride and Bad Pride

Pride is a vice that can turn a good, well-intentioned man (or woman) into an egotistical, gloating pig of a person very quickly. When we begin to think that all our talents, gifts, abilities, and skills are purely of our own doing, this becomes our undoing. Pride is what blinds us from seeing with true perspective who and what we genuinely are as human beings, as God's children — and it steals away the balance that we need to keep from falling flat on our faces, as we strive to walk the straight and narrow road that leads to our heavenly home.

At this point, some will naturally inquire: "Now wait a minute. What's wrong with pride? I'm proud of my kids. I'm proud of my work and my accomplishments. I have pride in my country. Are you telling me that's no good?" The answer to those questions is a loud, resounding "No!" There are two different kinds of pride. There is *good* pride and *bad* pride.

We can define *good* pride as a reasonable, justified, and balanced sense of joy, respect, and satisfaction in our (or another's) accomplishments and abilities. Good pride brings about a sense of value and contentment, and it is rooted in gratitude. This positive pride enables us to cherish and be thankful for the gifts we have been given. It helps us to bring about those accomplishments in life and to develop those abilities that enable us to perhaps do great deeds!

But, of course, there is a very fine line between *good* pride and *bad* pride, which is exceptionally easy to cross. *Bad* pride is an unreasonable, unjustified, and terribly unbalanced sense of joy and satisfaction in our abilities or accomplishments. It fosters a spirit and attitude of selfishness, arrogance, restlessness, ingratitude, and an over-inflated sense of worth. It leads to excessive ambition and a need to be idolized and unceasingly praised by others, and it also brings about a great overestimation of our own ability. In this case, negative pride is often referred to as *hubris* — and for the rest of our discussion, this is what I will be speaking of.

The Destructive Power of Pride: Playing God

We see a great deal about pride and its consequences in Scripture. In the book of Proverbs (16:18-19) we read, "Pride goes before destruction, / and a haughty spirit before a fall. / It is better to be of a lowly spirit with the poor / than to divide the spoil with the proud." These words certainly rang true regarding perhaps the most notorious and famous story of pride in history: the Fall of Satan. In the Bible, especially in the books of Ezekiel and Isaiah, we hear how Satan was originally one of God's most beautiful, loyal, and favored angels. However, he began to focus on his own magnificence, which was given to him by God. Thus, Satan eventually began to think that he was superior to God, and because of this pride, the Lord cast him out of heaven. Satan's "pride went before his fall" indeed!

I could go on and on, quoting Scripture passages here. But in essence, pride boils down to the same thing that Satan did: denying the superiority of God and worshiping one's self instead. It's this denial that can then evolve into a hatred of God and an aversion to all that is good. And remember: "Good" is the embodiment of life, love, and truth — all of which has its fulfillment and purpose in God.

In our current time, mankind seems to be full of pride more than ever, and much of that flows from the vice of greed, which we'll get to in the next chapter. How often we hear from the atheistic, "ethical" humanists of our day: "We are all gods!" In our culture, we see more and more how we attempt to "play God." Through artificial scientific procedures, many prospective parents seek to bring new life into the world exactly when they want, exactly how they want, and with exact attention to detail, as if they were designing and ordering a new custom home-theater system. And if there is the slightest potential flaw, abortion is readily available. How we forget that life is a precious *gift*, not a *right*, not something to selfishly "conjure," manipulate, or destroy as we see fit.

Then we have issues such as human cloning and embryonic stem-cell research (which differs greatly from truly productive *non-embryonic*, stem-cell research) that promises cures for the sick and hopeless but in reality only artificially creates life to use as parts, like a human junkyard, while lining the pockets of profiteering bioengineering companies.

Meanwhile, the vanity-obsessed shake their fists in defiance at the mirror as cosmetic surgeons stand by to nip, tuck, reshape, and slice and dice their bodies and faces into something that will meet the approval of the demanding fashion and body-image judges of the day — although tomorrow will bring a whole new set of physical criteria to meet. As botched procedures, life-threatening infections, and permanent damage ravage the bodies of desperate, tormented souls, the bank accounts of silicone-stuffing doctors continue to flourish and blossom. The "fountain of youth" is filled with blood and death, and pride is the source of its flow.

Now don't get me wrong. There is nothing evil in wanting to look and feel good (within reason), and the advances in medical science that have come about in recent years are truly amazing. They are a testament to the incredible ability that God has blessed mankind with. Such things have the potential to be harnessed to do an astonishing amount of good — to aid those suffering from birth defects or accidents, to cure diseases, to heal wounds, and to otherwise enrich our lives. But how often are such skills and abilities abused for prideful, self-serving motives?

How we certainly do enjoy "playing God." We want to recreate ourselves to look like *we* (or at least corporate Hollywood) want to look, despite how we were originally made. We want to create life in *our* image and likeness, not according to God's. We demand the ability to start life and destroy life at our beck and call, not at the invitation from the true Creator of life. We want to possess the gifts and talents *we* want — and we will do anything, no matter how destructive and vile, to get them whenever and however we want.

The truth be told, just like Satan, many of us do, in fact, want not just to *play* God, but to *be* God. And when pride manifests itself from deep within the recesses of our wounded psyche, and rears its ugly head, we insolently shout to the heavens, "This is *my* life! *I'm* in charge!" Yet all the while, we can't even cure ourselves of the common cold. And although one may exercise another ugly expression of pride in the form of assisted (or unassisted) suicide, we cannot, by purely natural means, add one extra second to the clock that counts down our earthly existence. And when our time is up and the lights of our mortality go out, we have no power to turn them back on. The truth is that life belongs to God, who has gifted us with it, and he is in charge. He is the potter; we are the clay.

The life that God has given us is full of potential and wonder. Something I bring up often is the fact that we are made in the "image and likeness" of God, which means that a loving God has made us out of love, for the purpose of giving and receiving love, and to do so out of love for him. And as St. Paul reminds us, without love, we are nothing (see 1 Cor 13:1-3). The Lord has also endowed us with a magnificent intellect and the gift of the will to use it. He has given us a mind, a body, and a soul to work in harmony, as we utilize another of his great gifts: the power of creativity. This gift of creativity has enabled mankind to build the Empire State Building; to design the Internet; to put a man on the moon; to compose timeless, breathtaking pieces of artwork; to invent the tools and procedures to perform brain surgery; and on and on. The ability to create and bring to life those creative plans is truly a reflection of the mind-blowing, creative power of God Almighty.

To have the audacity to take personal credit for the innate gifts that have enabled mankind to achieve astonishing greatness is the pinnacle of pride. We are only the recipients of these divinely designed abilities and talents that have been generously given to us. We are only the ones who have taken the initiative (as we should) to develop them and use them as best we can. And certainly, some have done a better job at this than others. Some have spent every waking moment honing and strengthening their talents and skills while others have lazily sat around and let their potential evaporate into thin air like the smell of a rotten tomato.

The Great Downfall of Pride

Once again, to be proud of the gifts God has given us and to be proud of the positive things we have done with them are good things. This is what *good* pride is all about. But as we've been discussing, it's when we think *we* are the ultimate source of all that goodness and greatness that we set ourselves up for that big fall, flat on our face, by means of *bad* pride. We see this phenomenon all the time.

I don't know how many boxing matches I've seen where the reigning world champion comes out before the fight at a press conference and boldly proclaims his superiority, carries on and on about how spectacular and unbeatable he is, and how perhaps he is the greatest pugilist that has ever lived — only to get cut down during the match like an old dead tree and take a brain-damaging beating from an underdog, no-name opponent. Ah yes, pride before the fall on live TV!

We see it time and time again: prideful athletes, musicians, celebrities, business professionals, scientists, and outdoorsmen (like our friend Mr. Boarman), all reveling in their self-crowned kingship, only to be humiliated beyond belief and knocked off their self-made throne in the most dishonoring manner possible. More recently we've seen record-breaking performances from athletes of various sports who are pathetically stripped of their glory months later due to their use of drugs and illegal performance-enhancers that they employed to pridefully maintain or achieve their "god-like" level of accomplishment. How our Lord's words ring true: "Whoever exalts himself will be humbled" (Mt 23:12).

As I mentioned, it's very easy to cross that line from *good* pride to *bad* pride — and it happens to all of us. It comes with just a subtle shift from reasonable, deserved satisfaction in a job well done to an undeserved, unreasonable gloating about it. It's the overstepping from a justified self-respect to an unbalanced, lethargically emerging self-glorification. Sometimes we don't even know we are crossing that line. Sometimes that satisfaction, joy, and respect we have in ourselves slowly grow like a cancerous tumor, which, in time, destroys the gratitude God ultimately deserves from us. If there is anyone to be proud of, it's God. He is our pride and joy. He is the reason for the goodness we have brought about. It is he who deserves our compliments of praise and glorification. When we are able to do great things with the gifts we have been given, be happy and rejoice — but most importantly, praise the Lord!

Pride affects us in many other ways beyond just becoming an egotistical braggart. It's because of pride that we fail to forgive others or to receive forgiveness for what we have done. Pride keeps us from admitting our sinfulness and our genuine inferiority (which we all have). Pride is what keeps us from seeking and accepting the help we need in life, whether it be financial, physical, mental, or spiritual. I run into lots of good people who have gotten themselves into bad situations, who desperately need help, but are just too proud to ask for it or receive it. They tell me, "I don't need counseling" or "I don't need to see a doctor" or "I don't need help finding a job" or "I don't need [fill in the blank]." In such cases, pride is disguised as personal strength and dignity, but in reality, it is weakness. It takes true strength to admit that one needs assistance. It takes great power to make the decision to be helped. As St. Paul said, "For when I am weak, then I am strong" (2 Cor 12:10). It's only by recognizing our faults, failings, shortcomings, and weaknesses that we can then realize that our strength is not of our own doing, but that it comes from the Lord.

Pride also builds many barriers in our lives and in our world. It puts up "roadblocks" and "barbed-wire fences" between people of different social classes, political parties, races, and religions. When pride takes over, we begin to think that we are too good to associate with the likes of "those people." We convince ourselves that they have nothing to teach us, that they are in some way inferior, that they simply don't measure up to the likes of us and "our kind." With pride in our heart, we look down our nose at the rest of the world as we sit upon our self-made seat of honor and distinction. And the longer we sit up so high, the harder we crash to the dirt when knocked off our "high horse."

Another area in which pride sneaks in and does its damage is in the realm of ethics and morality. It's because of pride that many in our society simply will not admit they are wrong in making an unethical or immoral decision. So often we justify ourselves and desperately attempt to intellectually let ourselves off the hook for the evil we have done by simply denying the objective truth of right and wrong, of good and evil. Pride blinds us and lies to us and deceives us — all the while convincing us that we are number one. Pride motivates us to rebel, just as Satan does, against what is true, good, and life-giving; thus, it paves the way for destruction.

Eating Humble Pie

So, what is the solution? Well, I'll tell you what it is: it's a huge slice of humble pie! The virtue of humility is the only remedy for pride. When we think of humility, what comes to mind for many is a preconceived idea of being meek, quiet, timid, and shy — and having an attitude of passiveness and never taking credit for one's accomplishments. Others associate humility with being humiliated — that is, with being terribly embarrassed. None of these is what true humility is all about.

True humility is what we have been discussing these last several pages: it's the recognition and conscious realization that we are creatures, not the Creator; that we are in need of God; and that it is he, and he alone, who has given us life and blessed us with the characteristics that uniquely define you and me. It is that which helps us form a true, brutally honest opinion of ourselves. Humility helps us disregard and cast aside the shallow quest for popularity and self-glorification.

Humility makes us true children of God. It helps us realize that we are dependent upon the Lord, for we cannot conjure out of thin air the dirt upon which we trod, the food that nourishes us, the blood that courses through our veins, or the water that hydrates our being. We cannot (naturally) add a single hair to our head or append another second to our life. It is not we who began the beating of our heart or the breathing of our lungs.

Humility helps us realize that there is always room for improvement in our life, and that we need God, just as children need their parents.

I previously mentioned a passage from the Gospel of Matthew that says those who exalt themselves shall be humbled. The other half of that verse is, "Whoever humbles himself will be exalted" (Mt 23:12). And so, it is humility that lifts us up in the eyes of the Lord. A man or a woman who is truly humble stands out like the North Star shining on a clear night. Their beauty, giftedness, and positive demeanor come beaming through with a quiet power, like the slight hum of a 10,000-watt sound system that could easily unleash a deafening sonic blast!

The humble man doesn't need to brag, because he knows what he's capable of. The humble woman doesn't need to desperately try to win the attention of others; she's well aware of her self-worth and dignity. Humble people don't need to shout their achievements from the rooftops or demand praise from others; they are satisfied with what they have been given and possess a healthy self-respect. And how truly refreshing it is to witness those individuals of enormous, unfathomable talent simply *not* saying and doing things to inflate their ego or pawn themselves off as a cultural icon. How wonderful it is to encounter someone of incomprehensible greatness who fully realizes from what initial source that greatness has come. The genuinely humble individual instantly earns our respect. Such virtue is cause for exaltation — not only in the eyes of God, but also in those of man.

The vice of pride can motivate us to eat up undeserved attention like a rampaging hog, seeking out every last morsel of ego-nourishing self-fixation. Pride fills our soul with a stink and filth, not unlike a waste-wallowing wild boar. It turns us into an overgrown, ill-tempered pig of a person. It is the virtue of humility that satisfies the voracious hunger of our soul; it washes us clean and tempers that hog-wild need for personal glory. When we have true humility, the animalistic, frenzied, aggressive nature of our sinful self is put to death. The pig of pride is slain, and the human being who is made in the image and likeness of God once again emerges and learns to truly live in the love and goodness with which we were created.

Chapter 4

TRICK OR TREAT!

THE CALL CAME THROUGH one dismal, rusty autumn day in 2005. It was my good friend, fellow outdoor fanatic, and brother priest, Father Greg Klump, on the other end. I noticed more than a hint of aggravation in his words as the static desperately tried to drown out his voice. But the bad news came through nonetheless: "The arrow rest on my bow is broken!"

I must admit I wasn't too surprised. In those days, there was a period of time in which Father Greg seemed to be consistently plagued by bad luck. There was just always a "black cloud" following him around, everywhere he went. But because this mechanical failure took place on the Thursday before the week of our big fall bowhunting extravaganza, it was very bad news indeed!

For those of you not familiar with the ins and outs of contemporary archery equipment, compound bows, like so many of our modern-day marvels, are a spectacular testament to man's ingenuity when they work properly — but at the same time, they can be a source of brain-bending migraine headaches when they do not work. When a major part fails or is out of whack on a high-tech bow, it can really do a number on the entire thing and render it a jumbled mess of impressive looking parts. And when the part is replaced or fixed, the bow often needs to be re-tuned and sighted-in once again, to ensure the pinpoint accuracy, blinding speed, and Godzilla-like knockdown power for which such a bow is designed. This can be a time-consuming task, especially for a priest serving in a parish with several thousand families.

Father Greg entered the doors of River Bluff Archery with that black cloud still hovering overhead. To make matters worse, the owner of the shop didn't have the replacement part that was needed to save the day. But then, a ray of sunlight dissipated the gathering cumulonimbus, as he found a nearly identical arrow rest in the storeroom. With haste, the kind owner swapped out the rests, which drastically cut down on tuning and sighting-in time — and to top it off, he would not accept any payment for his heroic display. He simply told Father Greg, "Bring me a picture." Was this a hint of hunting prophecy? Hmmmm . . .

With that matter settled, things were looking good as the weekend passed uneventfully, leading up to a Sunday evening rendezvous at deer camp. We were hunting on a 540-acre farm in Montgomery County, Missouri, and would have the whole place to ourselves for the better part of a week, thanks to the generosity and hospitality of the brothers who owned the land. That evening we planned our hunting strategies for the next morning, got all our gear readied, and tried to get some sleep, which doesn't come easily when one is bowhunting during the prime time of the archery season.

The "Trick-or-Treat Buck"

The bizarre images and strange happenings of my dream-filled head exited violently as the much dreaded, yet feverishly desired, electric snarl of the alarm clock shook me from my slumber. Through my blurry, tired eyes, I could barely make out the red glowing numbers on the clock's face. Groveling in the darkness like a blind, loathsome mole, I fumbled around for my filth-covered glasses, put them on my pillow-creased face, and finally made out the numbers: **4:00 A.M.** Gaining a little more consciousness, I suddenly realized: *Wait a minute. It's October 31st, and I'm going hunting. It's GO TIME, baby!* With the realization of where I was and what I would be doing, I instantly jumped out of bed, wolfed down some food, slammed a cup of coffee, took a shower, got dressed, and met Father Greg out on the front porch in full hunt mode!

Unbeknownst to me, Father Greg was not quite as enthusiastic as I was on that first morning. As he recalls:

> I wasn't in the most favorable mood for hunting. It was a warm fall, and most of the trees still had the majority of their leaves, when the woods would normally be nearly bare. Part of the reason, too, was that Father Joe would be occupying a much-coveted tree stand, from which he and I have seen many deer.

I didn't realize at the time that Father Greg actually wanted to hunt that spot. He mentioned the previous evening that he was going to hunt elsewhere, so I didn't think twice about taking advantage of such a great stand location. I know now that it was out of true kindness that he was graciously letting me have what would most likely be "first dibs" on a good deer for the day.

And so we split up, each making his way to separate parts of the farm to begin the first hunt of the week. Being fairly familiar with the location I would be hunting at that morning, I made my way there and got into the stand quietly, slowly, and efficiently. I was set up and ready to go in just a matter of minutes. The only thing I had left to do was wait until the sun came up.

Meanwhile, Father Greg was headed to a location known as the "Frog Stand," which was set just 12 yards (inside the woods) from a power line. Father Greg recalls what happened as the pre-dawn preparations unfolded:

> The problem I had that morning was that I only knew *approximately* where the stand was, but not exactly. I parked at one end of the power line and walked to where I thought the stand would be, but was unable to find it. Oddly enough, in the past this would have eaten me up

with frustration, but instead I just decided to not worry about it and wait till it was light enough to see.

As Father Greg continues to tell the story:

> While the light came slowly upon that overcast morning, I saw that I was only 60 yards from the stand after all and decided to empty my bladder where I was, before walking over to the stand. Once in the tree, I nocked an arrow and hung my bow on a screw-in hanger, arranged some gear in the stand, and then sat down to let the woods settle from my mild disturbance. I pulled out my cell phone (which was set to "silent" mode) at 7 a.m. and called Father Joe to check in, letting him know that I was finally on the hunt, and to find out if he had seen anything yet. He was in his stand about a half-hour ahead of me and had already seen three deer, including a year-and-a-half-old buck. I signed off, saying that I would call again later.

As Father Greg mentioned, I had deer all over me in those first few moments of sunup. I had two big does and a young buck come right into my area and actually walk directly below my stand. It was just a little too dim yet and I didn't have a good angle, so I let them all pass; I was holding off for a bigger buck, anyway. After that, nothing happened for a while, and so I did a little "rattling and grunting" (deer calling) to see if any bigger bucks were around.

After just a few hits of the rattle bag and a couple of aggressive-sounding "bbbgggggrrrruuup's" on the grunt tube, a much larger buck emerged from the edge of the clearing about 150 yards down the way. The deer showed himself briefly, looked over the area for the intruding buck he thought he heard, and then quickly went back into the timber.

Simultaneously, in Father Greg's neck of the woods, as he remembers:

While the time elapsed, I was just wandering in thought when, all of a sudden, movement along the power line caught my attention. A deer was walking toward me and was only 30 yards away. Immediately, I saw that he was a nice big eight-pointer. Unfortunately, I was caught totally out of position. I was seated, and my bow was hanging behind and over my left shoulder. He came right in to just 15 yards away and began making a scrape. I knew that I couldn't move or he would pick me off for sure.

The buck waited for a moment, then began to walk into the woods on my side of the power line, angling away. I decided I would let him walk away and then get into position and try rattling him back with a set of antlers I had with me. The buck, however, stopped at 25 yards and looked intently down into the valley away from me. I decided that I should try to stand and get a shot off. So I slowly stood up. But as I did, the deck of the stand buckled a bit. I was sure that he heard me, but he just kept looking for the "buck" that he thought was moving in on his territory. The truth is that he smelled my urine 60 yards from my stand and followed my trail, thinking I was a rival.

Meanwhile, back in my area, I decided to carefully get down from my stand and stalk through the edge of the clearing to a little patch of thick brush where I planned to set up and try a little more calling, hoping to close the distance some if the buck was still nearby. I stealthfully got into position, kneeling down in the cover of brambles and tall weeds, and did a few more grunts. Almost instantly, he popped out of the woods again, and this time jogged right down the line to where I was set up. My heart raced with excited anticipation and shock. I have to admit I was surprised that my plan actually worked!

As the buck got closer, I realized I would only have one chance to draw my bow without being spotted, and that would be when he came by a large set of oak trees that he was closing in on. When his head was behind the tree trunks, I drew back my bow and got into shooting position in a split second. As he emerged from the cover, he was standing about five yards from me, eyeball to eyeball! There is nothing as exciting as being at full draw on a deer at ground level! Wow! I've got goose bumps just thinking about it now!

As the buck stopped and looked at the clump of brush that also contained me, I realized that he was just not quite the caliber of deer to take, though still very tempting! (The rule of thumb for Father Greg and me, and for most of the places we hunt, is not to take a buck if it's not bigger than one you already have on the wall. We are not going to eat the antlers, so we like to let the immature bucks grow up; we take a doe instead, which also helps greatly with herd management.)

Still at full draw, with the buck staring me through, I slowly let down my bow and watched him bolt out of the area, slightly spooked by the strange movement he saw. My heart was still beating with excitement. Just to have such an encounter is a rare treat, and the experience alone was a "trophy" for me. As I got back in my stand for round two, I wondered what was happening with Father Greg.

So, what was happening with Father Greg and his buck? Something he'd been waiting a long, long time for, as he recalls:

> I finally got turned around in my stand and lifted the bow from its hanger, still amazed that the buck hadn't moved. Since the woods were silent and damp, I was afraid he would hear me draw the bow, but again he stood motionless as I came to full draw. I remember being relaxed and just talking to myself about the distance of the shot, saying, *He's farther than 20, but he's not quite 30.* So I split the difference, settled behind the right shoulder, and touched off the arrow.

The arrow found its mark, and the buck did a big mule kick as he exploded in alarm. About 10 seconds after the shot, I heard a muffled sound and wondered to myself if that could have been him falling. I replayed the scene in my mind and knew that the mule kick he gave was a tell-tale sign of a solid hit. I could see my arrow lodged in the ground where the deer had stood, telling me that the shot was a clean pass-through. Then all of a sudden, I just came undone. My whole body started shaking uncontrollably. I had been bowhunting for 19 years and have shot several deer with my bow, but I have been plagued with misfortune, missing four large bucks during that span. Years of disappointment were just erased as the reality of this hunt sank in.

With a beaming smile on his face, Father Greg goes on to tell the rest of the story:

I must say that I was excited about the hunt and how it worked out. But honestly, what followed next made it all worthwhile: sharing my excitement and God's blessing of the hunt. I called up Father Joe at 7:10 a.m., and he whispered a muffled "Hello" as he answered. With whispered excitement, I said, "Joe, I just smoked me a whopper!" He was surprised, and I suppose he was wondering if I was pulling his leg, as I have often done in the past when getting bored while on stand.

So I replayed the hunt and told him that the buck was likely down for the count. I climbed out of the stand, checked my arrow, and knew right away that the deer didn't go far. I backed out and went to meet Father Joe near his stand so that I could lead him to where I was hunting. I felt as if I were floating, as we walked into the woods to retrieve the downed buck. Unbeknownst to me, Father Joe was video recording the actual tracking and locating of the buck. I was filled with so much emotion when I finally saw the buck and lifted that beautiful rack. I can't express the gratitude I felt toward God for creating and allowing me to harvest such a fine animal, and certainly for being able to share it with my good friend, brother priest, and outdoor partner. And last, but not least, I was grateful that Father Joe is even stronger than me, because after pictures were taken we had our work cut out for us dragging the monster buck out of the ravine he ran down before expiring.

And to conclude this wonderful tale, Father Greg thoughtfully reflects:

> As I look back, a number of things came together to make the hunt work out and be enjoyable: the kindness of an archery professional, amazingly generous land owners, a good friend to share the gift of nature with, and a gift of the Holy Spirit that helped me be relaxed that particular morning. Some of the best gifts in life just come together in ways that you simply can't anticipate, but which leave us saying: "Lord, thank you for your greatness and letting us share in it." Oh, by the way, a few days later I walked back into River Bluff Archery to give the requested payment of the previous week, and the owner came out and asked why I was back. I just reminded him of his request: "You told me to bring you a picture!" He now has the picture hanging alongside a number of other nice trophies.

And so it was, at last, on Halloween of 2005, Father Greg pulled off a magnificent "trick or treat" on a mighty fine whitetail buck. His 19-year quest to harvest a trophy buck with his bow had finally been fulfilled. No amount of candy in the universe could have been sweeter than the success he rejoiced in that morning. But in the midst of this joyful story, there is a seedy darkness that emerges like a devil-masked Halloween prankster who is only interested in playing tricks and doesn't care about the treats.

Father Greg Klump and the "Trick-or-Treat Buck"

The Monster of Greed

To backtrack in the story some, when Father Greg called me at 7:10 that morning, as he mentioned, I didn't believe him. I said to myself, *Yeah, right. He just shot a huge eight-pointer. I'll believe that when I see it.* I was waiting for the punch line to what I thought was another of his morning hunt jokes, but it never came. There was just heavy breathing and silence on the other end of the phone after he told me what had happened. Then I realized it was for real. A shot of adrenaline bolted through my system with excitement for Father Greg harvesting his first big archery buck. But then, something happened that still haunts me like a dark night filled with ghouls, goblins, and ghosts.

After that initial excitement wore off, I experienced something that I thought I just didn't have in me. The malevolent monster of greed surfaced in my heart and bushwhacked the delight I was feeling for my bowhunting brother. Horrible, ungrateful thoughts began to pop into my head, such as, *Oh man, now I have to get down from my stand to help drag out a deer. My day is ruined! I wanted to get that big buck! My hunt is wrecked!* On and on the negative, pessimistic, selfish thoughts kept coming. I felt the burning sting of jealousy and envy tear into my heart. I was truly drowning in a stagnant, oily, stench-filled pool of greed.

After several minutes of internally, sinfully, self-destructing, I finally got ahold of myself and thought,

> *What the heck is wrong with you, Joe? This is one of the most joyful moments you'll ever experience in the woods! Father Greg is the guy who got you into deer hunting in the first place. He's the same guy who has graciously invited you along on countless hunts and sacrificed many a good spot to give you first crack at a nice deer. He's the same guy who gave up the better part of a morning to help you drag out your first big buck a few years back. How can you even think about being so greedy?*

After finally coming to my senses and putting those terrible self-serving thoughts out of my mind, I was able to help Father Greg trail, recover, and drag his huge buck out of the woods in the proper frame of mind, which was a spirit of charity and love. With very few exceptions, helping Father Greg that morning with his deer was one of the most joyful experiences I've ever had in the whitetail woods. I still remember it as if it were yesterday. And here the ecstatic bliss of that most wonderful morning was almost completely hijacked by the power of greed.

Yes, those few moments of being overcome by such terrible thoughts still haunt me. I just didn't think I had it in me. It was a startling and very unpleasant revelation to realize that deep down, I, like anybody else, can be a greedy son of a gun! As much as I try to be charitable and gracious in all things and at all times, especially in outdoor pursuits, I simply couldn't believe that I had a darkness in my soul, and that it would manifest itself as it did. But such is the allure of sin and temptation. No one is exempt from the sucking power of its tractor beam. It rears its ugly head when we least expect it and enters into us all. However, we have the power to accept it or reject it.

We can define *greed* (also known as *avarice*) as the immoderate, selfish, and excessive desire for things such as money, wealth, material possessions, food, success, and creature comforts. Now, obviously, everybody has a desire for money, food, success, possessions, and the like, to varying degrees, and there is nothing wrong with them in and of themselves. But when that desire is overrun by selfishness and leads to acts of injustice, dishonesty, ingratitude, and corruption, it is no longer a healthy, good desire. It's then that the monster of greed has emerged.

The Development of Greed

Greed is a downright ugly, nasty thing! And it seems to get us in its clutches at a very young age, which is all the more reason for parents to temper it in their children quickly, with diligent, disciplined, and loving guidance. All of us can recall that as youngsters there were those among us who often developed an insatiable appetite for more. Greedy kids want more toys, more cake, more candy, more cookies — more of everything that one could possibly develop a liking for. I can recall many a childhood birthday party where the alpha-kid of the day would shove his way through the gleeful, flailing arms of his peers in order to get to, and aggressively devour, all the pizza he could possibly shove in his mouth — not to mention also guzzling down the better part of an entire pitcher of lemonade before anybody else even had a fighting chance. And when it came to birthday presents, a truckload of gifts wouldn't have satisfied. Out of chubby, spoiled, ungrateful, overfed voices the motto of the day emerged: "I want more! I want more! Gimme! Gimme! Gimme!"

Of course, that first taste of greed manifested itself in many other ways, too. We most likely remember children who would

constantly jump in front of others and bully kids around in order
to always be the first in line at the amusement park or movie
theater. Those same kids, who were perhaps you and me, would
often cheat in games or on tests to always win, no matter what,
or to get the best grade possible. They would steal the nice things
that other kids had, or break them out of greedy spite. Sadly, in the
grand scheme of things, nothing changes much for many of those
individuals as they grow into adulthood. The attitude remains the
same: "Hooray for me, and to heck with everybody else!"

Our Greedy World

Every day the news is filled with stories of greed. We hear of the
shady dealings of certain insurance and pharmaceutical companies that fill their corporate pockets with gold, to the point of
bursting, while those who relied on them in good faith suffer.
Overpriced "wonder pills" can fail to bring healing and cause a
never-ending rash of side effects. Petroleum-industry price goug-
ers vacation on the beaches of the French Riviera while honest, hardworking folks go broke trying to fill the unquenchable,
thirsty gas tanks of their gluttonous vehicles just to get to work
every day. Drug dealers and pimps enslave and abuse desperate
souls — all in the quest of "getting paid" and adding another
gold wristwatch to their collection. There are CEOs who make
more money while they're going to the bathroom than any one
of their employees makes in a month. And we've all seen how
the greedy race for quick, easy, and huge profits can bring an
entire economy to its knees.

   We see again and again how greed influences the actions
of corrupt politicians, lawyers, policemen, health care providers,
and clergy who put blood money in the bank to build earthly
kingdoms on the foundation of the toil, mistreatment, and pain
of others. As I mentioned in the previous chapter, prideful professional athletes (at times "aided" or even pressured by their
coaches) greedily subject themselves to illegal performance-en-

hancers and wreck their health to be the "best," until liver failure or heart disease or another condition puts them, their titles, and their enormous bank accounts in an anxiously awaiting, over-priced grave.

The sickening stories go on and on.

The Sneakiness of Greed

While we sometimes think of greed as a "rich man's disease" and associate it with "those who have," rather than with "those who have not," greed does not discriminate. Greed can sneak up on all — the rich and the poor, the young and the old, the saint and the sinner. Like a stealthy Ninja in the night, greed can grab us around the throat and choke the charity right out of us in an instant. As I experienced that day in the deer woods, greed can come trailing behind the best of intentions in an attempt to sabotage even the purest of hearts.

We often don't even realize that it is happening — that greed is slipping past our built-in detector of decency. When someone solicits a donation for a worthy cause and we quickly reach into our wallets to generously give, there is sometimes that phenomenon of suddenly pausing, and then picking out a rag-gedy, stray, one dollar bill, instead of giving the twenty that we initially intended — all because we have just decided that the twenty would be better spent on the new *Jimmy-Fist** CD that we want. At other times, when someone asks us to help with one thing or the other, we will quickly commit to doing so, but then suddenly backpedal and come up with a flimsy excuse not to do it, on account of wanting to see the new "beat 'em up" action movie that has just been released.

And then there are those times that we do things when driving — like consciously running a red light — that endanger

---

* *Jimmy-Fist* is a term coined by Mr. Jason Weber (my catfishing buddy) that is used to describe fictional or actual dilemmas, difficulties, products, bands, food items, or almost anything that has no existing name.

ourselves, our passengers, and others, just so we don't have to wait another two minutes to get to our destination. In all such cases, where is the focus? On me, me, me! That childish battle cry emerges once again: "Gimme! Gimme! Gimme!"

The Remedy of Charity

And so the question arises: How, then, do we remedy this vicious vice of greed? The solution is found in the virtue of charity — or in this case, better described as *liberality*. The virtue of liberality has nothing to do with being "liberal" per se. It is properly defined as a spirit and attitude of generosity toward others. It consists of selflessly, lovingly, giving of one's time, talent, and treasure for the good of others. In exercising this virtue, greed is replaced with contentment. The burning desire to consume more, to get more, to achieve more, and to use more is replaced with a spirit of gratitude, service, and fulfillment.

As with any kind of physical exercise, exercising virtue is not easy — and if it were, it wouldn't do us much good or produce positive results. "No pain, no gain" is the mantra of many an exercise guru. And despite the "fast, easy, painless results" that the salespeople for cheap, plastic exercise gear promise us on late-night TV infomercials, that "pain" mantra holds true. If you want to get healthier, stronger, slimmer, or more muscular, then you *must* be committed to putting forth some serious effort. You *must* be committed to sweating buckets and pushing yourself to the limit, and beyond. I don't care what anybody says: that's the only sure (natural) way to success in the ways of fitness and athletic development. There simply will be *pain* (within reason), and lots of it, in order to bring about that *gain*.

So exercising and growing in virtue will be a painful process that requires tremendous exertion and maximum effort. In the Gospel of Mark, we read this:

And he sat down opposite the treasury, and watched the multitude putting money into the treasury. Many rich people put in large sums. And a poor widow came, and put in two copper coins, which make a penny. And he called his disciples to him, and said to them, "Truly, I say to you, this poor widow has put in more than all those who are contributing to the treasury. For they all contributed out of their abundance; but she out of her poverty has put in everything she had, her whole living." (Mk 12:41-44)

In this passage, we see what charity, or liberality, looks like: it's giving out of one's "poverty," not out of one's surplus; it's making a real sacrifice of one's time, talent, or treasure for the good of someone else; it's feeling some real pain so that someone else may experience a real gain. And again, it's doing all this out of a spirit of self-sacrificing love for others, which Jesus modeled perfectly. As Mother Teresa once said, "Do not tire of giving, but do not give your leftovers. Give until it hurts, until you feel the pain!"

Jesus had many things to say on the subject of greed and the need for liberality. In Matthew's Gospel, our Lord teaches:

"Do not lay up for yourselves treasures on earth, where moth and rust consume and where thieves break in and steal, but lay up for yourselves treasures in heaven, where neither moth nor rust consumes and where thieves do not break in and steal. For where your treasure is, there will your heart be also." (Mt 6:19-21)

How quickly we greedy humans forget, that after all our toil and efforts to build up our own personal kingdoms here on earth, when it's all said and done, *dust we are, and unto dust we shall return* (see Gen 3:19). It's only the treasure of heaven, which money can't buy, that really matters in the end. And so, "Take heed, and beware of all covetousness [greed]; for a man's life does not consist in the abundance of his possessions" (Lk 12:15).

To further make the point, we read this parable in Luke's Gospel:

> "The land of a rich man brought forth plentifully; and he thought to himself, 'What shall I do, for I have nowhere to store my crops?' And he said, 'I will do this: I will pull down my barns, and build larger ones; and there I will store all my grain and my goods. And I will say to my soul, Soul, you have ample goods laid up for many years; take your ease, eat, drink, be merry.' But God said to him, 'Fool! This night your soul is required of you; and the things you have prepared, whose will they be?' So is he who lays up treasure for himself, and is not rich toward God." (Lk 12:16-21)

Exercising Virtue

To burn off all that greed that has collected in our mind and heart, we have to exercise more and more the virtue of liberality/charity. When the temptation to be greedy comes, one simply has to do the opposite and be giving. Just as runners, by means of their will, *make* themselves go that extra mile, so we have to *make* ourselves reject greed and reach out in charity. Sure, sometimes it "feels good to give," but more often than not, in all honesty, it doesn't. And it's not about us *feeling* good; it's about us *doing* good — and doing so out of genuine love of God and neighbor, even if that "neighbor" drives you crazy at times. Real love is a conscious decision to sacrifice; it's not a pleasant, fleeting, and often deceiving, "feeling."

It's in this continuous exercising of virtue, and avoidance of vice, that enables us to build up *soul* power. Putting our faith into action helps us "walk the walk," and to "put our money where our mouth is." It's in doing this that we also build up the Body of Christ.

In his first letter to the Corinthians, St. Paul speaks of the Church as the Body of Christ. He proclaims:

> For just as the body is one and has many members, and all the members of the body, though many, are one body, so it is with Christ. For by one Spirit we were all baptized into one body — Jews or Greeks, slaves or free — and all were made to drink of one Spirit. . . . [Indeed], the parts of the body which seem to be weaker are indispensable, and those parts of the body which we think less honorable we invest with the greater honor, and our unpresentable parts are treated with greater modesty, which our more presentable parts do not require. But God has so composed the body, giving the greater honor to the inferior part, that there may be no discord in the body, but that the members may have the same care for one another. If one member suffers, all suffer together; if one member is honored, all rejoice together. Now you are the body of Christ and individually members of it. (1 Cor 12:12-13, 22-27)

As St. Paul points out, every part of our own physical body has a function and a purpose, each part is very different and unique, and each part relies on the others for the body to function as a whole. So, too, each of us has a function and a purpose as part of the Body of Christ, the people of God. Each of us is different and unique; and just like our nature as individual human beings, when one part of the body fails or is harmed in some way, it negatively affects the whole.

God has blessed each of us with particular gifts, talents, and personality traits. As much as one may try to become a carbon copy of another, we were made, and will always be, specifically our own person. Just as we each have a completely original set of fingerprints, so also we each have a completely original soul. Each one of us is a masterpiece of God's creation, although many don't live out or even try to develop the incredible potential that lies dormant within. Thus, just as the parts of the human body work together as one, so we, too, as God's people, are designed to work together as one.

We are each called to use the gifts and blessings we have been given to spread the Gospel message, to live in and share the love of God with others, and to build up and strengthen the Body of Christ — and each of us will do that in different ways. You may be able to positively affect the life of someone in a way that another person might never be able to do, and vice versa. But the key is to recognize, develop, and be grateful for what you *can* do, not what you *can't* do or what someone else can do. Enviously focusing on the gifts and talents of others only tears down the Body of Christ with ignorance, bitter jealousy, hatred and, of course, one of the most destructive agents of all: greed.

It's in graciously giving that we receive. It's in helping someone else in their weakness that we are strengthened. It's in doing our job as just one part of a body that we enable the whole to function properly and do amazing things. It's in putting to death the monster of greed that the fire of self-serving egoism is extinguished. It's the virtue of liberality that truly liberates us to live in freedom as God's children, and to fully give and receive the great gift of his empowering love. And this is the only gift that keeps on giving!

Chapter 5

RIVER OF ENVY

I HATE THE SUMMERTIME here in the Midwest. There is absolutely nothing about that time of year that I look forward to, at least now that I'm not in school and don't have anything like a three-month vacation. I've never understood why so many people long for those miserable months, or why there are so many whimsical songs praising that most dreadful season. I detest everything about it! It's just hard for me to be positive, and that's for several reasons.

First, there is the constant inhalation of disgusting, bacteria-ridden, germ-laced, recycled air that blasts through the air-conditioning systems of buildings and vehicles — everywhere! The constant transition from the searing heat of the sun to the freezing, meat-locker atmosphere of so many places of business or recreation makes me ill. I just can't seem to adjust. It baffles me how folks complain of the cold during the fall or winter, yet during the summer they have the thermostat set so low that icicles practically form inside their homes or cars.

Besides the miserable heat and drowning humidity — which is even worse for a guy who wears black polyester most of the time — there are a multitude of foreboding, menacing, hostile threats that await one in the outdoors. Honestly, I'd much rather come face-to-face with a man-eating grizzly than come into contact with the poison ivy patches that grow as big as 18-wheelers around these parts. Despite my almost fanatical, paranoid precautions, I end up itchin' and scratchin' all summer long. If I were to head to the woods in an astronaut suit, I'd still manage to catch a nasty batch of that horrible stuff. My skin crawls just thinking and writing about it. Yikes!

Along with the many oozing, itching, rash-inducing plants that grow everywhere in the good ol' summertime, there is a host of tiny, and even deadly, insects just waiting to make one's fun in the sun a living hell! Hordes of ankle- and shin-biting chiggers are standing by, hiding out in the tall grass, just waiting to pounce and feast on one's hairy (or not so hairy) legs! Swarms of mosquitoes hover in the thick, damp air, slowly buzzing ever so closer, moving in carefully toward a big throbbing forearm vein to suck a pint of blood and leave one infected with the West Nile Virus.

Tiny deer ticks are peppered all around warm backyards, hiking and biking trails, overgrown shrubs, and virtually anywhere else they can find to ambush their prey, which includes you and me. Oh, they long to dig themselves deep down into your waistband or burrow into your backside, as if they were mining for gold! And once there, feasting on your flesh and blood, there is a rather good chance they could leave you with all kinds of sickness, including the potentially fatal Lyme disease. Toxic bug repellents that can melt the plastic off a cheap digital watch are the only wellspring of hope and source of defense.

To add to the summertime fun, how about going for a pleasant stroll through the park, merrily singing songs, whistling Dixie, and watching the passersby while enjoying a big, frosty, double-scooped ice cream cone? Sounds great, right? Well, while that creamy delight rapidly melts into a handful of sugary goo, the wasps, bumblebees, and hornets home in on the sweet smell and come blazing down upon you like F-16s, piercing their painful stingers into your candy-coated skin. You swat them away in an arm-flailing frenzy, but it's no use — it just provokes them more! And when you're brought to your knees by the insect venom running through your central nervous system, the fire ants come a-marching to finish you off as you lie there in agony on the burning blacktop!

To make matters worse, when you muster the strength to get up and run home, a swarm of hungry, thumb-sized horse-flies pick up on the commotion and zip down upon you, sinking their fat fly faces abysmally into the back of your sweaty, leathery neck. Ouch! Once again, the more you swat and fight, the more aggressive they get. Your only hope is to smash them with your bubblegum-coated, silly summer shoes in a fit of defensive rage!

I won't even bother mentioning the poisonous snakes, garden-destroying pests, house-wrecking termites, life-choking weeds, or other critters that thrive and flourish during those splendid months. You get the point. Summer? No thank you, friend. You can have it all! Sure, one could spend free time staying inside, watching TV all day, or lazing around a pool, soaking in the cancerous rays — but that's just not for me, either.

The Time-Honored Float Trip

Even though, as you can clearly see, I hate that time of year, I still get outside and try to make the most of it. I'll do some deer scouting, tree-stand hanging and maintenance, weed whacking, trail clearing, outdoor archery practice, fishing (of course), and the occasional float trip. If one is going to be outside during those miserable Midwestern months, it might as well be in a canoe, somewhere in the shade, floating down the cool, refreshing waters of a spring-fed river, creek, or stream. One still has the usual outdoor summer hazards to contend with, but if things get too bad, one can always abandon ship and dive in the water for protection and rejuvenation.

The time-honored "float trip" is a great way to explore new territory; scout out fishing, hunting, or camping spots; do some outdoor photography; spend time with family and friends; or just plain relax and have some fun. Even if one is not a skilled canoeist or kayaker, he or she can always plop down on a raft or an old tire inner tube and float along the river carefree, letting the current do all the work.

Exploring new territory

Float trips provide the opportunity to experience the otherwise unseen beauty of particular areas. These trips also offer a chance to view all sorts of wildlife in their natural state, as they come to the waters for food, hydration, and refreshment. Every creature on earth enjoys spending time by the water. It is a life-enriching source for all.

Like anything else in our world, though, there are always a few who ruin something nice for everybody. This, too, is an unfortunate reality for quite a few float trippers. Oftentimes, the backwoods and waters that provide otherwise peaceful escape and sacred solitude become the haunts of hooligans looking for nothing more than trouble.

Rivers and streams that usually offer sanctuary from the workweek and the hectic commotion of life are (during the summer) commonly transformed into Ancient Roman-like madhouses, with pimple-faced punks using the parking lot like an ancient vomitorium. Beer bongs loaded with cheap golden swill and cut-rate cigarettes are clenched tight in the hands of overweight, bikini-clad (or sometimes topless) gals and their rail-thin, emaciated, meth-addicted boyfriends. Vulgar cursing, maniacal laughter, loud music, and the smell of burning brain cells fill the air. (By the way, I'm not trying to offend anyone here; this is just the way it is. Nothing but the facts, folks!)

This sort of thing, thankfully, doesn't happen on *all* rivers *all* the time, but it is quite common. Such an environment is a much-dreaded sight for the family that drove three hours and was hoping to have a nice quiet day on the water. As marijuana smoke wafts through the air, and beer cans and fistfuls of cigarette butts cascade down the clear waters around one's feet, a sense of disgust rises to the surface of one's soul. The good news is that, more and more, this kind of behavior is not being tolerated, and that local authorities are diligently cracking down on it in many areas.

Because of this aggravating atmosphere, I limit my float trips these days to late summer, when most people are done with their vacations (or are in prison) — and I try to avoid the weekends as I would the Black Plague! I can vividly recall one such weekend trip when it was prime time for such craziness; it was a "hooligans' holiday," you might say.

Observations From a Canoe

On that particular float trip, I was on a river way down deep in southern Missouri, which is an incredibly beautiful domain that I've always greatly cherished. It was an area far, far removed from pretty much everything, out in the middle of nowhere. I was quite shocked when, while out in this extremely rural location, the day began with the disturbing sights and sounds that I previously described. There was no escape from it the entire day. Around every bend, and on every sandbar, beach, riverside clearing, and parking lot, there was absolute bedlam and chaos!

As I drifted along in a beat-up aluminum canoe, trying to ignore all the noise and insanity, I began to notice something: there was a striking similarity in all the rowdy folks I encountered that day, besides their banefully obnoxious activities of choice. Almost all of those individuals were trying to be something they were not, and attempting to be somewhere they certainly were not.

All of these rural, country dudes who were gathered in the parking lots had gangster rap booming out of their old, burned-out pickup trucks — and out of their mouths. They wore their baseball hats cockeyed and their pants backwards, almost hanging down to their knees. (Again, I'm certainly not trying to offend anybody here; I'm simply describing the facts of what I observed.)

The groups of people that were hanging out on the sandbars and such also had their bass-heavy radios blaring filth-ridden hip-hop, while they danced about and carried on as if they were in a decrepit, bombed-out club somewhere in Chicago, New York, or L.A. There wasn't a tucker hat or a pair of cowboy boots to be found anywhere, nor was there a Lynard Skynard or Hank Williams, Jr. song to be heard along the river that day. It was a forced, ridiculously obvious, deliberate exchange of one social stereotype for another.

The Nature of Jealousy: "Everybody Wants What They Don't Have!"

At one point along the way, my buddy in the front of the canoe turned around, smiled, and said, "How true it is: Everybody wants what they don't have!" It was a river of envy. Everybody I saw that day was clearly envious of another lifestyle, another people, and another culture that was far removed from their own. And as desperately as they tried to enter into the fantasy facade they created for themselves, it was comical — yet downright sad, really — to witness it from an outsider's perspective.

This phenomenon is certainly nothing rare, though, and it takes place virtually everywhere. People who come from a sparse, meager upbringing often want wealth and abundance, while those who come from wealth may desire a much simpler life. An infertile couple desperately desires children, while a couple with plentiful fertility deals with it as if it were a disease. A heavyset person wishes he were 50 pounds lighter, while an ectomorphic young man consumes weight-gaining protein shakes by the gallon! The star athlete (secretly) wishes he had better grades and possessed a higher IQ, while the brainiac is envious of those who possess such magnificent physical abilities. The talented artist wishes she had the financial know-how to better make ends meet, while the banker longs for the gift of creative expression. The small-town girl dreams of Broadway spotlights, while, at the same time, a celebrated actress is about to lose her mind from the pressure, wanting nothing more than to live someplace where nobody knows her name. The scenarios go on and on. People want what they don't have. Envy can easily rule our mind and heart.

Envy — or jealousy, if you prefer — can be defined as an anger, pain, or sadness that is rooted in someone else having the things we want for ourselves. Those "things" could be talents, skills, material possessions, relationships, careers, living conditions or geographical location, good fortune, or just about anything else one can think of. You name it, and somebody is envious of it.

St. Augustine once said that envy is "*the* diabolical sin," and that "from envy are born hatred, detraction, calumny, joy caused by the misfortune of a neighbor, and a displeasure caused by his prosperity" (see the *Catechism of the Catholic Church*, no. 2539). That's a powerful statement!

Now granted, one could find theologians, philosophers, psychologists, and all sorts of smart people who would say that some other vice is *the* major sin that leads to all others. Some would say anger is *the* sin that is the root of all others. Another would say that greed, not anger, is the archetype for all vice. As we have seen, and will continue to see, any of the seven deadly sins can be the catalyst and launching pad for the other capital vices that wreck our lives and blacken our souls.

That being said, envy certainly is intimately related to the vice of greed, and also to that of lust. Envy is rooted in the desire for the goods of another, while greed is the hoarding of those actual goods that have been (or will be) acquired. Envy is also related to lust in that both flow from covetousness — but lust zeros in more specifically on a disordered desire for self-gratification and pleasure. More about that later.

Let's backtrack a bit now and take a closer look at that statement of St. Augustine's: "From envy are born hatred, detraction, calumny, joy caused by the misfortune of a neighbor, and a displeasure caused by his prosperity."

How true this is! As I've already hinted at in the last couple of chapters, time and again we hear the awful stories of athletes, performers, and corporate hotshots and such, who, out of a nasty, bitter envy of others' talents or positions, sabotaged those people in the most hateful manner possible to get their positions, their salaries, or the esteem of others which they possessed. The anger, pain, or sadness that flowed from *not* having those things boiled to a head and overflowed into violent, undermining, malicious actions to get the things they envied so terribly.

The "detraction" that flows from envy can be seen everywhere, from kindergarten classrooms all the way to retirement homes. When we, of any age, become jealous of another, we are often prone to belittle that person as much as possible. Degrading, disparaging, and damaging comments erupt, like hot lava from a great volcano, out of the mouths of the envious toward the target of their jealousy. This detraction that comes from envy is what is responsible for many of the labels we put upon others. As I mentioned earlier, truth be told, the "geek's" intelligence is greatly desired; the "jock's" athletic ability is longed for. And if we can't get or achieve those things for ourselves, then we badmouth that person and his or her ability all we can, in order to pathetically make ourselves feel superior.

When our hateful, detractive comments don't seem to faze those we envy, we may resort to "calumny" — that is, starting all manner of fiendish rumors to ruin someone's good reputation as a way to make ourselves look better by contrast. If we can't have what another person has, then by golly, we can make his or her life miserable in one way or another! "Did you hear what so-and-so did? Sure, she's bright and beautiful, but she did [fill in the blank]! Can you believe that? See, she's not so great after all! I'm better than she is!" Again, we unfortunately witness this kind of behavior among all ages, from two-year-olds to elderly grannies and grandpas in wheelchairs.

The only source of joy for the miserably envious person whose being is bubbling with anger, pain, or sadness is the misfortune of the person who is the target of his or her envy. The "geek" picks up his bulbous, big-eared, brainy head from behind his trigonometry textbook and, through Coke-bottle glasses, watches with delight and lets out a throaty, horse-like, weaselly laugh as the "jock" gets tackled by someone twice his size on the football field and gets his knee dislocated. On the other side of town, a big meathead "jock" — who, in reality, won't make the NFL and will work in fast food for the rest of his life — pins down a "geek" to the locker room floor and slathers hair-removing foam all over his victim's pencil-necked head so that everyone in the school can laugh and torment him for weeks to come. Once again, in all honesty, both desperately desire the other's abilities, but never, under any circumstances (including the threat of death), would they admit it in the light of day — that is, unless they've consumed the better part of a 12-pack.

The envious wife, in a fit of depression and dissatisfaction, runs up debts that neither she nor her underemployed husband will ever be able to pay — all because she *has to have* just as good of (or better) furniture, appliances, clothes, jewelry, and entertainment gadgets as her neighbor. The envious husband, motivated by the same displeasure over his own material and financial status, maxes out all the credit cards so that he can get a bigger home, faster car, and higher-definition TV screen than the guy who lives across the street. And when it's all said and done, the satisfaction that is so badly desired, the things that are coveted so intensely, do not, and will not, satisfy for more than a short spell at best. The end result is living on borrowed time and borrowed money in one's self-made kingdom on earth, which crumbles as fast as it is erected. The hard, cold truth is that all the money in the world, all the material possessions, or anything else one covets will not satisfy the envious heart.

Envy and the Undertow of Ingratitude

Like a primordial wrestler desperately scrabbling to overcome his opponent, the vice of envy "throws" gritty, blinding "sand" into the "eyes" of our soul. Jealousy keeps us from recognizing our own talents, gifts, worth, and uniqueness. It robs us of a humble appreciation for who we are and how God created us. It takes away the joy and gratitude we can, and should, experience in life and, in turn, serves us up a big envy-enchilada. And then, after wolfing it down, we only get a terrible case of spiritual and emotional indigestion — no satisfaction. As Rocky Balboa would say, it makes one "mentally irregular."

Like any one of you reading this book, I have also grappled with the vice of envy. When I was in high school, I was terribly envious toward anybody who could lift more weight than I could in the gym or play the guitar better than I could. There were a couple of people around school who fit that description, and I secretly hated them! Even though they were, in fact, decent folks, at the time I perceived them as cross-faced villains who were out to ruin my life, who always had smug looks on their faces, as if they were mockingly lording their abilities over me for all the world to see!

I'll admit that I reveled in hearing the ridiculous, untrue rumors about them that would circulate around school from time to time. I thoroughly enjoyed joining in conversations that tore them down and rubbed dirt in their faces. Though I never really told anybody, or made a big outward public display about it, I just couldn't stand the fact that they were better than I was in those areas. I would engage and participate in any little passive-aggressive tactic I could think of "to get back at them." As time went on, I eventually got over it and moved on to being envious over other things in life. But no matter what it was, the results were the same: emptiness and dissatisfaction.

Things changed one day after school, when I took a good, long, brutally honest look into the mirror of my psyche and said to myself:

> You know what, Joey ol' boy? You will *never* be the world's strongest man or win the Mr. Olympia contest. *Never!* However, you will always [God willing] have the innate potential to be physically strong, pretty darn healthy, and in relatively good shape. So thank God for that! Many would do anything for good physical health. You will *never* be voted "Guitarist of the Year" or play in a platinum-selling rock 'n' roll band with millions of adoring fans. *Never!* But you will always be able to play guitar, create music, and share it with others. Thank God for that!
>
> You may not *ever* [notice I didn't say *never*, hehehe!] catch the world's record brown trout, but you have vast opportunities to enjoy the outdoors and pursue the things you so passionately love. So stop whining ... and thank God for that!

As the years went on, and I entered college and later the seminary, I continued to implement the occasional stone-cold reality check to keep myself humble, grateful, and spiritually in tune. I do the same thing today, regularly. When I find myself getting down, I call to mind the fact that I have friends, family, shelter, food, health, education, talents, transportation, opportunities, and all kinds of things going for me that people in other parts of the world would literally kill for! Sure, like anyone, I have things that bring me down, struggles that depress the heck out of me, and crosses to bear that seem too heavy at times. But in the grand scheme of things, I have *NOTHING* to ever be sad about, dissatisfied with, or envious of — and I dare say that holds true for most of you reading these words.

Life can be rotten and miserable at times, and things are far from perfect, but the simple truth is that things *never* will be perfect. That being the case, I count my blessings daily and live the life God has given me, with what he has given me. As I often say: For every one thing that is going wrong in one's life, there are dozens that are going right, for which one probably has never even said, "Thank you."

Those reality checks keep me well balanced these days. Even though I firmly believe and advocate the notion that we can accomplish virtually anything we put our minds to, and that we can far exceed what we (and others) thought ourselves capable of, we do need to realize that there are some things that simply will not ever happen, period! This is so true . . . *unless* — and I repeat, *UNLESS* — God sees fit to bestow on us the opportunities and blessings that empower and allow us to achieve what was previously, and truly, impossible. And that does happen. God is good! Those gifts are given by no merit of our own; they are signs to us of God's goodness, presence, and power. But we have to receive them with a humble, grateful heart.

Who knows? Maybe the Good Lord will, in fact, bless me with that record brown trout one of these days!

Fraternal Charity: An Attitude of Gratitude

This more positive, satisfied mode of thinking flows from the virtue of fraternal charity, which is the remedy for the vice of envy. *Fraternal charity*, which is sometimes referred to simply as the virtue of "kindness," is a gratitude for one's talents and gifts, as well as, and more importantly, a gratitude for the talents and gifts of others. This virtue also embodies a genuine desire that others will bring to completion the potential they have been given as human beings and children of God. It's the virtue that a good coach or hunting/fishing guide must possess.

A successful coach does not sit on the sidelines fuming mad with a heart full of envy because he was never as good as his star player. Instead, a good coach has a positive, grateful appreciation for the talents his players possess. He wants to see them develop their potential, to exercise the talents they have, and to work hard and diligently to be successful. And if and when that success comes, he shares the joy of victory with his players as if he were out there on the field himself.

A good hunting or fishing guide is much the same. An experienced, honorable guide does not brood with jealousy and plot the ruination of his client if that person catches a bigger fish or harvests a more magnificent animal than he ever has. The guide, instead, is filled with joy and satisfaction from using his knowledge and talents to direct those of his client, and to bring about something truly spectacular, most memorable, and infinitely satisfying.

Fraternal charity is what clears up our spiritual vision and helps us to truly see. (Remember that from Chapter 1?) Through the eyes of kindness, we see the value of things for what they are, and we develop an attitude of gratitude for them, instead of being consumed with envy.

We recognize someone's ability to ace test after test as a genuine gift. We see another's capacity for physical excellence as a true blessing. An individual's incredible ability for artistic expression is recognized as a divinely bestowed asset. As discussed earlier, we humans are all made out of the same stuff. But for whatever reason, we are all unique; we are all given different talents; and we were all given them for different reasons. They all give glory to the creator and giver of those gifts: God.

The virtue of fraternal charity changes one's outlook from "Dang! I wish I could do that! I hate that person for being so good at that while I stink so bad!" to "Wow! What amazing talent that person has! What a gift! Praise God!" Fraternal charity enables us to appreciate the delight and beauty that the gifts of others bring into the world and into our lives, while also enabling us to be grateful for our own talents, and to develop and use them the best ways we can.

Watching Bill Dance catch huge bass and Will Primos harvest massive whitetails brings great joy into my life, while at the same time making me aware of my own outdoor inadequacies. And I'm perfectly fine with that. Listening to Eddie Van Halen or Steve Vai rip on the guitar sends sonic shivers down my spine and fills my ears with auditory bliss, while also making me realize I could practice to eternity and never even scratch the surface of their musical prowess — and again, I'm perfectly fine with that.

As a priest, something I'm constantly made aware of from my insights into the lives of others is that, quite often, those we are envious of are actually envious of us. As we've seen, we often want what we don't have — but if we were to get it, if we were to switch places with another, we'd be jealous of what we used to have. The cycle goes round and round, and it only ends when we stop frantically paddling down the violent waters of the river of envy and instead learn to fraternally float with the charitable currents that flow from an attitude of gratitude.

Chapter 6

SEEING RED IN THE LAND OF THE MIDNIGHT SUN

OUR PLANE TOUCHED DOWN in St. Louis at 11:32 a.m. Vacation was over. My hands were ripped to pieces from line cuts and hook gouges. My forearm and hand muscles were sore, stiff, and still locked in an iron-claw death grip from the almost nonstop handling of heavy salmon rods all week. There was no point-less, lazy, lethargic lounging about on sunny beaches, sipping cocktails all day on this trip (nor on any of my vacations for that matter). I was exhausted beyond words from sleep deprivation and seemingly endless activity — but I loved it!

I gasped from shock as Father Greg Klump and I stepped off the plane, out into the 100-plus-degree Missouri summer heat. Just 24 hours earlier, we were fishing in Johnstone Bay next to a glacier, delightfully freezing half to death. Humpback whales were leaping out of the salty, turquoise waters of the Pacific Ocean. Several dozen brown, fat, blubbery sea lions were sunning themselves on a big jagged rock in Resurrection Bay. A lone grizzly bear roamed the water's edge looking for breakfast, while we drifted along in search of coho salmon in a most wor-thy fishing vessel called the *Mighty Moose*, captained by Father Greg's brother, Phil. (If you're ever in the Anchorage area and need an outstanding dentist, give Dr. Phil Klump a call!)

As we picked up our luggage and headed for home, my heart was heavy with the reality that it was finished. My third and best-ever Alaskan fishing adventure had come to an end. As I'd experienced in the past, I did not want to leave, and I immediately thought of going back, somehow, someway, as soon as humanly possible.

I again felt as though I was leaving behind a significant chunk of my soul. As much as I love (and I don't use that word lightly) my home state of Missouri, I also have a burning, passionate love for Alaska. The beauty of Missouri is intimate, tamable, and captivating. But the wild, massive expanses of the Alaskan wilderness and waters are beyond comprehension. It is truly "the last frontier." It demands respect. It is not tamed, nor should it be. It has claimed the lives of many an ill-prepared, uneducated outdoor enthusiast and naive nature lover. Alaska is no place to fool around. It is not Disneyland! It is a domain of tooth, fang, and claw. It is a place where Mother Nature displays her unbounded beauty in all its glory, but also where she manifests her brutal, savage indifference to life and death. Survival of the fittest reigns supreme.

As we left the airport and went our separate ways back to home and parish, I immediately began reflecting on the week's events.

It all started on a Monday, as Father Greg, Mike James, and I drove from Anchorage to Soldotna to fish the Kenai River. The well-ridden RV, graciously provided by Phil and his family, was to be our home and transportation for the week. (By the way, it would not be possible for me to go on these Alaskan fishing trips if it were not for the hospitality and generosity of the Klump family. I'm eternally grateful.)

As we drove along the Sterling Highway, I found myself wanting to take a picture of virtually everything I saw. Stunning snow-capped mountain peaks reached heavenward, as Dall sheep roamed the rugged hilltops. Majestic bald eagles reverently soared about in the cool, thick, ethereal air. Pristine emerald-green trees of various species blanketed the landscape. Brilliant violet fireweed decorated the roadside vegetation. The deep grayish-blue waters of creeks, lakes, and rivers flowed freely through the valleys and meadows, like veins carrying blood, supplying life to all.

The three-man Alaskan fishing machine! Left to right: Father Joe, Father Greg, and Mike James

Everywhere I looked I saw breathtaking, indescribable beauty and grandeur that would have made a magnificent postcard. I wanted to wrap my arms around all that I beheld. I wanted to bodily diffuse, vaporize, and let my soul forever rest and meld into this paradise. All that I perceived reflected just a hint of the magnitude of the glory of God.

In Search of Salmon

Several months of preparation, and the better part of a day spent on planes and in airports, were all about to pay off in the start of a weeklong adventure when we at last arrived at our first destination, Centennial Park, where we would camp out and fish for the first day or so. After quickly organizing our site, we frantically suited up in our waders, rather hurriedly got our gear together, rigged the stout fishing rods up with our hand-tied salmon flies, and with tremendous haste made our way to the fast-flowing water of the legendary Kenai River. It took us a little while to get the hang of the proper drift/swing fishing technique once again, but after several dozen casts we were back in the saddle.

The most common method of fishing for red (sockeye) salmon along the rivers is to attach a large fly to a fairly long leader, attached to a generous chunk of lead, which, in turn, is attached to the main line. The rig is then gently cast, or flipped upstream; it bounces along the bottom of the river, back toward the bank in a swinging motion, and then the process is repeated. Sockeye salmon, while being the strongest swimmers and toughest fighters, are often called "shy" salmon because they rarely strike a lure (or a fly) out of an aggressive feeding instinct like other species of salmon. Reds feed mainly on plankton, so when one fishes for them with rod and reel, it is more a matter of trying to snag the opened-jawed fish in the mouth or to coerce it to hit the fly in an attempt to simply get it out of their way.

Because of the red's general lack of "biting" the fly, one has to be constantly aware of any nominal hesitation or bump in the presentation. When the slightest interruption occurs, the hook must be set — and set hard! Many times that "bump" or hesitation will be due to running over a rock or underwater debris, but at other times it will be because of the slight mouthing of a sockeye. And when that hook is set, all "shyness" goes out the window! Pound for pound, the red salmon dishes out the fiercest fish battle on earth! A hooked sockeye, which generally weighs in at 4 to 16 pounds (16 pounds being the current record), will leap several feet in the air, make line-burning, skin-searing, knuckle-busting, rod-snapping, arm-breaking runs, up and downstream. It's truly like hooking into a speedboat — or an underwater freight train! The fight those fish can dish out is absolutely incredible. It's like nothing else on earth. It's an almost frightening experience at first. It just seems unfathomable for a fish to produce and display that much power.

One reason the salmon fights so hard is because it is on a mission of life and death. A salmon's life begins in the autumn when its mother deposits eggs into a gravel bed, which are then fertilized by the male. The egg gives way to various stages of development and eventually becomes a young fish. The little guy will then either migrate thousands of miles to salt water or spend another year or two in the freshwater lake or river where it was hatched, before heading out to sea. After spending several years out in the ocean, millions upon millions of salmon will begin their journey home to the river of their birth, to spawn and die, thus completing the cycle of life.

The salmon lives its entire existence in constant danger of being killed. Rainbow trout, Dolly Varden, and similar fish feast on salmon eggs during the spawn and continue eating them as the salmon develop into fry and smolts. Diving birds such as mergansers, loons, and kingfishers also take their toll on the newly hatched fish. When the salmon grow up and move on to the open sea, they become the prey of sharks, lingcod, halibut, seals, whales, dolphins, eagles, etc.

On its journey home during the spawning run, the salmon faces a never-ending gauntlet of challenges and obstacles. Commercial fishing nets, anglers, natural and man-made obstructions of all kinds, bears, and other predators constantly pose a looming threat. But the salmon carries on, guided by his almost supernatural sense of smell, over thousands of miles through violent, turbulent, churning waters to get to its place of origin, to regenerate new life and then die.

As the salmon get closer to their spawning grounds, they undergo a spectacular and rather creepy metamorphosis. The breeding male sockeye salmon, for example, develops a long mean-looking set of hooked jaws, with big, sharp, flesh-ripping teeth, topped off by a fearsome hump on his back. Male and female sockeyes both turn a brilliant scarlet red, which intensifies as they get closer to home — hence the nickname "red" salmon. During this time, the fish are actually in the process of dying, using up all energy, nutrition, and bodily reserves to complete their unbelievable, monumental journey to their place of birth.

As I mentioned, upon the completion of this aquatic pilgrimage, the fish spawn and then die. But even after their death, as millions of fish carcasses lie rotting on the banks of streams and rivers, filling the air with a pungent stink, this, too, is a source of life, as the nutrients from these dead fish flow into the water and nourish their sons and daughters, sustaining their contribution to new life.

Combat Fishing

And so, there we were, Father Greg, Mike, and I, lined up like salmon-fishing soldiers on the front lines of the battle, knee-deep in the cold waters of the Kenai River, casting relentlessly to the incoming reds that were fresh in from the sea. Again and again we cast our rigs upstream, carefully tuning in to the vibrations coming down our fishing lines, waiting for that elusive tap on the other end. It wasn't but a few minutes when I suddenly felt a bit of excessive drag in my drift. I half-heartedly set the hook, thinking I was just hung up on the rocks below the surface. But as I lackadaisically reared back on the rod, an outrageously maniacal explosion, like an underwater depth charge, erupted just a few feet out of the water in front of me! As I muttered the customary "Fish on" proclamation in shocked disbelief, a big healthy sockeye flew out of the water like an MX missile taking off at full speed! And just that fast, the hook dislodged and the fish was gone. Mike and Father Greg gave me an intense, knowing, confident look, as if to say, "Well, all right. The reds are in, baby!"

As the afternoon progressed, we each hooked into several fish, but were not able to land most of them. For every four or five hookups, we'd land one fish, which is not too bad of an average, really. Hours passed and the action was rather slow. Over and over we'd flip, drift, and swing, flip, drift, and swing: cast to the 1 o'clock position, swing at the 10 o'clock position, cast to the 1 o'clock position, swing at the 10 o'clock position. My shoulders burned from fatigue, and my hands were locked in a "death grip" — and I'm no limp-wristed sissy! It was very physically demanding fishing.

We carried on for quite some time, and just when we were about to call it a day, a sudden flurry of activity kicked in. It seemed that a major "slug" (a large group of migrating salmon) was coming through. We started hooking into fish (and landing many of them) left and right. With a burst of extra confidence and adrenaline, we carried on. Finally, eight hours later, closing in on midnight, we decided to call it quits for the day and hit the hay. As we cleaned and filleted our fish and headed back to camp, Mike broke the silence of our meditative zone and confirmed our insanity: "I don't know anybody who would have fished for eight straight hours like that and not said a word of complaint!" I knew then that this would be a stellar week: we were a three-man, unstoppable fishing machine!

The next morning I awoke at 6 a.m. to find the RV empty. Mike and Father Greg were already on the water, and had been since 4:30! I quickly got myself together, shoved my trademark peanut butter sandwich down my throat, chugged a soda (no time for instant coffee), and headed to the water. We fished till around 11:00, added a few more fillets to our collection, pulled stakes, and headed to our next stop, the Russian River, which was just a hop, skip, and jump from the renowned Cooper Landing area: fish Nirvana!

The Russian River campground is yet another outdoorsman's paradise, complete with a good supply of grizzly and black bears. All around us were warning signs about bears and instructions on how to keep one's campsite bear-free. I realized it was no exaggeration, when, upon arrival at our spot, we discovered a very large, rather fresh, bear claw mark imbedded in the pine tree right outside the door of the RV.

Though the Russian River is full of gigantic rainbow trout and salmon of all different species, the fishing was rather slow, with the exception of Father Greg hooking into a mighty fine specimen of king salmon. It was quite an exhilarating sight to see a massive, blood-red beast of a fish (in the 30-pound range) leap out of the water at full throttle! Unfortunately, Father Greg was not able to land that fish, but it was still an unforgettable thrill for all.

Later that evening, after partaking in a fantastically delicious meal of fresh grilled salmon, we sat around camp, and each just drifted off to his own world of thought. It was then that another specimen of wildlife emerged: the great North American Jackass. This creature walks on two legs instead of four, and is known by his or her excessively loud vocalizations and inconsiderate displays of rambunctious behavior during times when it would/should be peaceful and quiet. After the ruckus finally died down, the exhaustion of the day kicked in and all were fast asleep.

The sun rises quickly in Alaska — heck, it hardly sets for that matter — so the next day we were up and at 'em before the cock had a chance to crow. We all were especially looking forward to this day, as we would be doing a float trip down the middle Kenai River. Armed with heavy-duty, 9-weight fly rods, our guide took us through the calm, serene waters of Skilak Lake and eventually into the river. More majestic bald eagles perched in high, lofty, rugged limbs, stoically on the lookout, as we slowly moved by in the big blue drift boat. The mirror finish of the lake's surface was interrupted only by the slight breaching of salmon on the move. I fully expected to see a moose or two come down to the water's edge for a morning sip, but none showed up.

After a wonderful trip through the waters and woods, we finally landed the boat, lined up a few yards off the bank in the river, and began fishing. Again, things started off slow. It was the same old routine: flip, drift, and swing, flip, drift, and swing. Cast to the 1 o'clock position, swing at the 10 o'clock position, cast to the 1 o'clock position, swing at the 10 o'clock position. Suddenly, things picked up and the peaceful calm of the morning turned into a sockeye salmon free-for-all. "Fish on! Fish on! Fish on!" We were hooking and landing fish so fast and furiously it seemed unreal! The air was filled with the sounds of excited fishermen, with the smack of salmon being bludgeoned over the head with the fish billy-club, and with the abrasive sound of sharp knives slicing through the gills to bleed the fish out (which makes for a cleaner, purer fillet). In no time at all, our stringer was loaded to the hilt with a three-per-man limit of marvelous sockeyes.

After the fish had been cleaned and squared away, we drifted farther down the river in search of the monstrous, world-famous, 30-inch rainbow trout that inhabit these waters. No new world records were set that afternoon, but I did manage to land a nice two-pounder as a result of our efforts. As the day came to an end, we packed up our gear and headed back to camp. On the way there, Mike drew our attention to a big black bear that suddenly emerged from the woods, ran down to the river, grabbed a fish in its mouth, and headed back to the thickets so fast that the fisherman just 20 yards away didn't even see what happened! Wow! What a spectacular display of predation, efficiency, and stealth! It was our first Alaskan bear sighting of the trip!

Deeper Into Alaska

That evening as I sat by a small fire and sipped a couple cold ones, I reflected more deeply on what we were actually doing here. Our experience of fishing in Alaska (or anywhere for that matter) is far more than mere "sport." It is a catalyst for journeying to distant, captivating, terrifically beautiful lands and becoming active participants in the cycle of life, side by side, with the rest of creation.

We were not just mere spectators, not just ungrateful recipients — like so many who have no idea where their food comes from or the price it paid to make it to the dinner table — but true stewards of the precious resources that have been entrusted to us. All around there was life and death, consumption and renewal: bears, moose, eagles, fish, people — all striving to sustain life, to renew life, and to live life here in this dwelling place of surreal vitality.

The next day, after a final walk along the ever-captivating Russian River, we packed up and headed back to Soldotna to fish another portion of the Kenai, this time while staying at Swift Water Campground. As we had experienced a few days earlier, the fishing started off slowly, but picked up quite a bit in the evening. What was to be a relaxed session of fishing turned into another eight-hour, nonstop shift of wrestling with the mighty sockeye salmon.

After the fish were cleaned and all was done for the night, I once again sat outside for a while to wind down, pray, and reflect on the day's events. As my exhausted eyes gazed into the thick, neck-high brush surrounding our campsite, and as I listened to the hypnotizing sounds of the rushing water from the river below, I began hearing rustling and popping noises coming from back in the brush. I sat up a bit more alertly and noticed the dense weeds shaking and small trees snapping just 20 feet away. It was unusually dark for an Alaskan night due to the thick cloud cover, and so I couldn't make out what was causing the commotion.

I noticed a fading plume of smoke from the neighboring campsite and thought perhaps someone was out collecting kindling wood or dry brush to reignite a campfire. Suddenly, a large dark shape slowly reared up from where I was hearing the noise. More than causally alarmed, I mentally exclaimed, *Good gravy!*

It's a gargantuan bear! He must have gotten a good whiff of all this fish and has come for dinner, with me as the appetizer!

I instantly snapped out of my malaise, slowly got up, took a few more steps back in the direction of the RV, and then shined my flashlight on the mysterious hidden creature. Thankfully, it wasn't a giant man-eating grizzly bear, but it was a Herculean-sized moose! I watched in cautious awe as this monstrous beast casually came out of the brush, right into our campsite just a few yards away, and continued to browse around in the vegetation. After a few more doses of my flashlight and the commotion of Father Greg and Mike coming outside to have a look, he moved on down toward the river. Wow! Yet another unforgettable Alaskan encounter.

The next morning started early with a repeated bout of fishing on the part of Father Greg and Mike, but I sat this round out. The exhaustion finally caught up with me, and I decided to sleep in a little to recharge my batteries in preparation for the final leg of our trip: fishing for silvers (coho salmon) in Seward. As we loaded up and hit the road, I felt more rejuvenated and was getting fired up once again. During the better part of the two-hour trip to our next stop, Mike was out cold, the exhaustion finally catching up with him as well. After taking in yet more of the resplendent Alaskan terrain during our drive south, we eventually made it to camp and met up with Phil and his family for dinner.

With stomachs full of hearty Northern cuisine, the rest of the evening was spent helping Phil get his boat ready and making the necessary preparations for the next morning. That morning came very quickly, and at 5 a.m. we were up and at 'em again with military-like quickness and efficiency — Phil had been in the Army, after all! After launching the *Mighty Moose* from the harbor, we had a little over an hour-long boat ride to get to our destination for the morning: Johnstone Bay.

Those long boat rides, which became a part of the daily ritual for the three final days of the trip, took on a special, divine nature for me, and also for Mike, I suspect. While Phil, Father Greg, and the rest of the crew sat inside the cab of the boat, Mike and I sat outside on the fishing deck toward the back of the vessel for those raw, cold, and at times, spine-jarring rides on the big water. Sitting back there seemed to lessen the blows of the heavy-duty, impacting seas. But more notably, being out in the open back there, taking it all in as we motored along, became an unforgettable, meditative, and metaphoric experience. It was the perfect setting for my daily hour of undisturbed prayer that I try to get in no matter where I am.

The vast mountaintops kissing the sky, the endless ocean stretching out to the horizon, and the vaporous clouds emitting from the nearby glaciers were like incense rising heavenward. The seabirds that drafted along in the air behind the boat, our breathing in the fresh salty air, the breaching whales, the bears walking the distant beaches, the almost chant-like hum of the engines — all became the sacred sanctuary for my time of prayer. As I mentioned, I try to get in an hour of undisturbed prayer every day — a "Holy Hour," as we Catholics call it. As a priest, I pray all the time throughout the day, but having a solid, unbroken daily hour is an absolute necessity, and those rides out to the bay became the perfect time and setting for that hour with God.

Those trips became metaphoric in that they seemed to mirror the journey of life toward eternity. As we left the noise and hustle of civilization in the harbor area, I felt as though I was leaving the entire world behind. As the protection and comfort of the surrounding lands and communities receded farther away and we headed out to the open waters of the Pacific Ocean, it was as if I was being transported to another dimension. Out there, there was no bitter division of political parties. There was no angry, irrational feuding over theological or philosophical issues — they didn't amount to a hill of beans out on the high seas.

Nowhere to be found were the mind-numbing, nonstop distractions from electronic gadgets and entertainment appliances that stare us in the face and shout in our ears at every waking moment of the day. There was no intellectual currency being wasted on the hedonistic, soul-rotting rantings of Hollywood celebrities, rock stars, or pop therapists. There was nothing but the raw manifestation of God's power and creation. Everything else was "dust in the wind."

Out amidst the big rolling seas and the uncontrollable waters, I felt the true intimidation of the absolute dynamism of nature. It's something I don't experience much in the wilds of the Midwest, or anywhere else. Out on the sea there is only you, your captain, your fellow crew members, and the vessel upon which you dwell. We weren't all that far from land, but still, in the grand scheme of things, we were like a leaf floating on the open ocean. It wouldn't have taken too terribly much for something to go wrong, with us sinking to a watery grave. But with faith in the *Mighty Moose* and our captain, we headed on through a time and space filled with primordial magnificence.

For me, the journey of life is much the same. It's a conscious leaving behind of negative cultural stimuli, heading out beyond the comfortable confines of affirmative and not-so-affirmative societal expectations and norms. It's a constant process of emptying myself of distractions and heading to a destination not often visited by many of our modern-day materialists: the vast wilderness of the soul. In this place, there is nothing but an overwhelming, humbling awareness of the divine, of one's own littleness, weaknesses, vulnerabilities, and sinfulness. There is also the urgent need for the love, the guidance, and the presence of God. Such an experience makes me realize that God is my captain, my fellow man is the crew member, and my mortal body is the vessel which carries me to the joys of eternity — though that joy will not be fully realized until I get there . . . and hopefully I will get there!

In the same manner, the joys of those trips out to Johnstone Bay were not fully realized until we got there. Those cold, clear waters yielded some of the biggest, most beautiful silver salmon I've ever seen. The fun and excitement of fishing with the rest of the gang was absolutely fantastic! The breathtaking natural decor of our surroundings was far beyond alluring. The fight that those chrome-plated, sterling silver-looking coho salmon served up was a fisherman's dream! The experience was genuinely reminiscent (though minuscule at most) of what it must be like in heaven.

Captain Phil Klump and a bundled-up Father Joe
with a hefty coho salmon

When we think of heaven, we can't imagine it without our favorite activities and our favorite people. Those are the things that bring us the most joy, satisfaction, and love in our lives. But on a much deeper and more significant level, as my good friend Father John Pecoraro often points out, God is the source of those things, and so the fun of experiences like catching massive fish, the pleasure of exchanging a laugh and a smile with loved ones, and the captivating beauty of the natural world are all just teeny-tiny hints of the joy, the satisfaction, and the love of being in the eternal, uninhibited presence of God Almighty. Nothing we can possibly ever imagine will come even remotely close to the grandeur, joy, and love of seeing God face-to-face! It is an eternal bliss that will go far, far beyond the pleasure of any mere human activity we may now enjoy and think we can't do without.

On the last day of our trip, and the final day of fishing Johnstone Bay, I asked a special request of God. As I reflected back on the week and all that I'd thought about, meditated upon, and talked about with the Lord in prayer, I simply said: "God, you know I'm not one to ask for signs and such: your presence is all around me, and I clearly recognize it. But if you see fit, would you let me catch my largest fish of the trip this morning to confirm all I've experienced this week with you?"

And sure enough, my final and last fish of the day and of the trip was in fact a behemoth silver salmon, in the 12- to 15-pound range, that almost ripped my arm off as he valiantly fought his last fight. After I landed the fish, got a few photos, and placed it in the holding tank, I once again gazed heavenward, smiled, and said, "Thank you, Lord." I have no doubt that the Good Lord was smiling down on me, and whispered in the wind, "You're welcome, Joey ol' boy."

When we were done fishing, I sat back on the deck for the ride home, chewed on some peppered moose jerky, and tried to say good-bye. When we got back to camp, we had to load up fast and move out quickly in order to get everybody, including Father Greg and me, to the airport on time. Before Phil took us to the check-in gate, I celebrated Mass at his home. It was the perfect end to our Alaskan adventure. As we gathered around the large wooden dinner table and celebrated the Lord's presence in word and sacrament, I was reminded that this is our cycle of life. Jesus is where we start and where we end. He is the beginning and the end. He is the source and the summit of our lives as Christians. All week long I'd been hunting for God in the magnificent woodlands of that ruggedly handsome land. All week I'd been fishing for the Lord in those stunning waters. But there, at the celebration of the Eucharist, at Mass, we were experiencing his true presence in the most real and profoundly sacred way on earth. And so, with our souls nourished by the Word of God and the Bread of Life, we said our good-byes, boarded our planes, and headed home.

Ahhhhhh. Just thinking about that trip still fills me with a deep longing to get back up there. My heart truly aches for Alaska. I just can't stand to say good-bye! As I said at the beginning of this chapter, I feel as if I've left behind a chunk of my soul. But it'll be there next time for me, God willing!

An Alaskan Nightmare

To take a step back for a moment, all that I've described and written about in this chapter up to this point has revolved around the perfect fishing trip, or at least as close to perfect as one could get: the perfect place, the perfect conditions, the perfect company, the perfect experiences, and so on. But let me tell you, such has not always been the case. I could have easily filled the pages of this chapter with the tale of an Alaskan fishing *mis*adventure. It was perhaps one of the most depressing and miserable experiences of my outdoor career! I don't like to think about it much, and I don't want to spoil all that I've just expressed, so I'll give just a quick summary.

My first trip to Alaska was a bittersweet nightmare! It was sweet in the sense that I was, well, going fishing in Alaska, which is something, up until then, I had never dreamed possible — much less would I have ever fathomed being able to go back several times since. Alaska was, and is, the ultimate fishing destination for me and countless others. Once you've been there and experienced all, or even some, of what she has to offer, you can die a happy man/woman!

When the realization sank in that particular year, that my greatest fishing fantasy would become a reality in the upcoming summer, I was stoked with excitement and exhilaration beyond words. It's all I thought about for months. I was obsessed! I had visions in my head of rivers so thickly packed with salmon that one could walk across the water on their backs. I dreamed of landing 90-pound kings, 12-pound rainbows, dozens upon dozens of reds and silvers, and frolicking merrily with all the majestic wildlife in a great euphoric celebration of life. I conjured up images of nonstop action, with everything going perfectly according to plan and as right as could possibly be!

Well, this is where the "bitter" part comes in. The majority of everything we expected and proposed to do on that trip went as horribly wrong as possible on that first trip to the Land of the Midnight Sun. Now, please don't misunderstand me: to just be there and finally see and experience the natural beauty of that spectacular land was as captivating as could be, and it was way beyond my wildest expectations. To have been invited by Father Greg to go in the first place, and the hospitality of Phil and his family, was truly humbling — and again, I'm forever grateful. But I'll tell you what: it was genuinely mind-blowing as to how many things turned into a semi-disaster on that trip. It was as if somebody was out to get us!

The weather was extremely windy and nasty, even by Alaskan standards, which put the kibosh on several of our planned outings. The boat that Phil had at the time, which was much smaller than the *Mighty Moose*, broke down twice, and half the trip was spent driving back and forth to Homer for repairs, and then waiting for those repairs to be completed. And as a result of all those heavy hauling drives, the bearings on the trailer went kaput! The guided fly-out trip we had planned for one of the days was canceled due to more bad weather, and the little bit of fishing we did do in Soldotna, along the Kenai, was so unbelievably, painfully slow that it just made me want to cry!

On one of our few seemingly trouble-free rounds of fishing that week, I suffered the aftermath of another unexpected situation. Before we headed out to halibut fish one day, I took Phil's advice to take some Dramamine, to avoid getting seasick. Now, I've never had a problem with sea or motion sickness, so I was hesitant. But after listening to Phil's stories of otherwise tough, hearty souls vomiting their brains out as if they had a belly bursting with botulism, I thought I'd better heed the warning. Well, thankfully, I didn't get sick — but wouldn't you know it, I did get so darn drowsy from the Dramamine that I really could not keep my eyes open, which is extremely rare for a guy who suffers from insomnia most of the time. I had to lie down in the cab of the boat so that I literally didn't fall asleep and fall overboard! That stuff knocked me out of commission for the rest of the day.

To top it all off, on the last morning of the trip we decided to cough up a few bucks and hire a charter boat in Seward to take us out fishing for silvers. As luck would again dictate, we ended up on what was indisputably the slowest, oldest boat in the entire harbor! As we chugged along out to Resurrection Bay, even people in kayaks were passing us at times! To make matters worse, one of the other fishermen on the boat with us was an older gentleman with a stainless steel hook for a right hand, who was perhaps the meanest, grumpiest, orneriest son of a gun I've ever met in my life. He kept barking orders at the guides, yelling at everybody, and complaining about virtually everything, nonstop. Even when he kicked back to take a little snooze on the miserably apathetic two-hour boat ride out to the bay, he had a permanent mean-looking scowl branded upon his face!

We did manage to catch a few fish on that horrible venture — but even then, one of the deck hands, who was just an inexperienced kid, was given the task of cleaning and filleting our catch, and he was butchering the heck out of them! (One has to start somewhere, and we certainly didn't blame the young lad for giving it his best, and it was great to see his youthful enthusiasm. But thankfully, Father Greg offered to give him a hand and saved our hard-earned fish from being sliced to inedible pieces of dog food.)

I could go on and on with more details, but you get the point. Aside from taking in the unforgettable sights of Alaska and being introduced to this heaven on earth, that vacation was a total disaster!

Seeing Red

It was in the midst of that trip that I found myself getting far beyond angry. I was so dang, cock-a-doodly, sandblasted, darn mad that I felt I was on the verge of exploding like a great Alaskan volcano — which there are many of, by the way. I was downright wrathful, and the object of my anger and wrath was God.

It all boiled to a head around the fourth day of the trip, as I recall. I was standing hip-deep in the Kenai, casting away, over and over again, all the while in a brooding, stewing silence, begrudgingly thinking about all that had gone wrong already — and still we were not catching fish. Finally, I looked heavenward and silently had it out with the Lord. In my heart and mind, I began screaming at the Almighty:

> *All right, what in the heck are you doing to us down here? You know, I'm never too upset about what happens on a fishing trip, if I catch fish or not, and that kind of stuff . . . but this is ALASKA, darn it! This is different! This is the Super Bowl of fishing that I've waited for all my life! I may never get this chance again! And what do I have to show for it? NOTHING! Nothing but miserable mishaps, and not one lousy stinking fish! NOT ONE FISH! Here there are hundreds of thousands, millions even, of big feisty salmon moving through these waters,*

and I can't catch one! What are you doing to me? I demand that you let me catch a fish! That's it! You better listen to me, God!

And wouldn't you know it, the second I finished my pathetic, self-indulgent rant, my fishing rod was almost ripped from my hands as the water erupted and exploded with an aquatic fury and a huge red salmon blasted out of the river, and like a horizontal flash of lightning, bolted upstream in one mad rush! I was so shocked by the whole event that I just kind of stood there as the powerful fish ripped several dozen yards of line off my reel and eventually got free. In the heart-pounding aftermath, I again just stood there in disbelief as I heard the Lord say in my heart, *There! Are you happy now?*

I was truly ashamed of my loss of temper and my display of ingratitude. Like a spoiled child, I'd been selfishly screaming and yelling at my Father, while he stood by patiently, with a slight smile on his face, all the while knowing what was best for me and helping me to finally realize it.

Later that evening, back at camp in Ninilchik, as I sat outside and overlooked the waters of Cook Inlet, I realized the gravity of my ingratitude. I had let the anger of my unfulfilled expectations get the best of me and sour the experience of being in that incredible place. And even though things were not going as *I* wanted, it was still an extraordinary blessing to just be there. That alone, just being in Alaska, is something that thousands dream of, but never get to actualize. As I peered up through the comforting confines of my hooded sweatshirt, I saw an eagle soar overhead and was reminded of a line from John Denver's song *Rocky Mountain High*, which said that a man would be poorer if he never beheld an eagle flying.

I didn't have much in my wallet, or in the bank back home, but I was, and still am, a very rich man indeed! The Lord has blessed me far beyond my wildest dreams — and ashamedly, I just didn't recognize it, and even greedily asked for more. Forgive me.

Anger and Wrath

Once again, as in times past, my unfulfilled expectations were the cause of my unbridled wrath and anger. I addressed this topic a little in *Hunting for God, Fishing for the Lord*, and as I mentioned, expectations play a big role in our lives. When they go unmet, if they are unrealistic or misguided, they can become the root of enslaving vices and the cause of many of our difficult struggles. When we are honest with ourselves, we see that we have specific expectations regarding how quite a few things in life should work out. And when they don't work out according to plan, we get angry, and we often express that emotion, which in and of itself is perfectly healthy and normal, in ways that are not so healthy and normal.

Almost all of the initial expectations or desires that we have are at the very core good ones. But when we fail to meet those underlying expectations and fulfill those primary desires in holy and healthy ways, we then fulfill them in unhealthy and unholy ways: we sin.

Many people desperately try to fill those voids with a variety of things that are simply not good, with excesses of all kinds: too much food or alcohol, drugs, stimulants, pornography and other sinful sexual activities, and on and on. Those who cannot deal with a particular family member or situation at home often become workaholics or engage in various types of avoidance behavior. Individuals who have great difficulty with someone at work or school may find themselves acting out in passive-aggressive ways, doing all sorts of mean little things to get back at that person instead of having an open and honest confrontation or discussion about it. Whatever the situation is, if it's not being dealt with in a good way, then it's most certainly being dealt with in a bad way, which only perpetuates the problem.

As I stated earlier, most of us have a few different areas of vice, sinfulness, or moral struggle that we seem to deal with week after week, year after year. And as many spiritual masters have suggested, we all seem to have one primary sin or vice that we gravitate toward, which leads to other vices — although we often do not even realize it's happening. Lust can lead to various forms of gluttony. Envy and pride can lead to greed. Gluttony can lead to sloth, greed, etc. Any one major vice can kick off a chain reaction leading into other dangerous areas.

Anger, though, is perhaps one of the most common sources of ignition. A common thought process that goes on deep within the psyche is something like this:

> *I'm so darn angry (though I'm not totally sure why, and I don't know how to deal with it) that I deserve (pride) to take it out by comforting myself with a huge fatty meal (gluttony), with the pleasure of the sexual sin of my choice (lust), with taking a long, excessive break (sloth), with buying more things for myself (greed), etc.*

To take a more in-depth look at anger, again keep in mind that it's not necessarily a bad thing. As St. Paul says, "Be angry but do not sin; do not let the sun go down on your anger, and give no opportunity to the devil" (Eph 4:26-27). So it's not so much anger, but what we do with it, that leads to sin. Anger is an emotion we were created with, which we all experience. It is a natural, hard-wired response to something we perceive as an injustice or a threat of some kind, either toward ourselves or others. Even Jesus got angry. In the Gospel accounts, we hear how Christ became very upset with the money changers and "businessmen" in the Temple who had turned God's house into a den of thieves — and so, quite physically, the Lord drove them out (see Mt 21:12-13; Mk 11:15-17; Lk 19:45-46; Jn 2:14-17). It was a justified reaction and a legitimate course of action by the Son of God in response to what was going on.

The vice, or sinfulness, of anger is not the emotion itself in its natural, pure form, but instead the "wrath" (as referred to in the original seven deadly sins) that comes from our expressing anger and acting on it in unhealthy, unholy ways. In the midst of our anger, the threat or injustice we perceive, which has sparked it, may not be, in reality, a threat or an injustice at all — or, at least, not nearly to the life-threatening degree we think it is. Oftentimes, our angry, wrathful reactions are based on mis-information, misunderstandings, and our own skewed, unbal-anced perception. The nature of these subjective, inappropriate reactions can flow from a variety of causes, such as one's particu-lar upbringing, abuse, mistreatment, and social conditionings. Because of these elements, we often overreact, blow up, jump off the deep end, take things way too personally, or say and do things we later regret terribly, such as acting out in violence. Our passions can easily get the best of us, and out comes (or in goes) a blazing wrath of destruction!

Like the other emotions we experience, anger varies in degree and also manifests itself physically with things like an elevation in blood pressure, an increase in heart rate, sleeplessness, and headaches. The source of our anger can be from others we know and deal with directly or indirectly; from conflicts within our-selves; from memories of past events; from "stubborn," inanimate objects while on the job; or from a host of other sources. But no matter the cause, when anger comes, we do one of three things: (a) we express it, (b) suppress it, or (c) try to ease and calm it.

Virtuously Dealing With Anger and Wrath

Psychology tells us that the healthiest way to deal with anger is to express it in an assertive, yet non-aggressive way. What this essentially means is that we need to recognize what is mak-ing us angry, clearly identify it, and then deal with it and seek a just resolution in a healthy, respectful, rational, constructive way — not in a vengeful, destructive manner, as so many do, which only makes other people angry and starts a whole new cycle of wrath.

When anger is suppressed, it is done so by being ignored, covered up, and turned inward, which usually leads to things like depression, abusive behavior to self or others, or a multitude of other negative physical and mental conditions. It is possible, however, to suppress and then redirect the energy from anger into other (more constructive) uses, such as exercise; but for this approach to be of value, we have to be able to clearly identify what we are angry about and decide if there is a readily accessible solution. There is grave danger in not being able to identity the source of our anger. It's then that it stews and broods and eventually turns into a monster! When we are angry about something that we simply have no power over, like bad weather or mechanical breakdowns ruining a fishing trip, this redirection can be a healthy method of coping, along with just plain calming ourselves down, taking a few deep breaths, and deciding to stop being a big baby!

There are a lot of angry people out there, as we all know. Anger is a way of life for many in our society. More than a few Internet chat rooms, blogs, forums, and message boards are loaded to the hilt with incredibly angry, truly ignorant people who have found no other way to deal with their wrath than to unload it on unsuspecting victims by means of the World Wide Web. Highways and streets all over the country are flooded with fist-shaking road-ragers who just can't get over the fact that the light turned red a little before they would have liked, or that somebody accidentally cut them off. Many teachers, ministers, employers, politicians, social activists, and professionals of all kinds try to cholerically express the importance of their work by falsely validating it with the seal of unwarranted wrath — and in the end, they hurt mostly themselves and their message by taking such a route.

Men, especially, have a tendency to think that anger is the only acceptable emotion to display. Some don't think it's manly to express sorrow, confusion, affection, or joy; but, by golly, they can get mad as hell and thoroughly enjoy showing it! Crazed angry coaches and dads (and moms, too, for that matter) will scream and yell and fight till kingdom come at Little League baseball games, for all the world to see, and think they are exhibiting their team spirit in dramatic, bold fashion, when, in reality, they are showing their severe lack of sportsmanship by their severe lack of self-discipline, self-control, and temperance. Any hotheaded fool can shoot his mouth off and blow his top — two-year-olds do a great job of it!

Uncontrolled anger is like a huge pot of boiling water: it won't stop cooking until the fire at the base is put out. Anger simply will not go away until it is dealt with in a healthy manner. It will just work its way into other areas of our life, transform itself into some very ugly behaviors or habits, and tear us down, bit by bit.

In the process of constructively dealing with anger, one of the first steps is to change the way you think (and when I say "you," I'm including me!). Instead of letting your passions get the best of you, take a step back, calm down, and use your brain. Replace your extreme, exaggerated thoughts with rational ones. Address the situation as objectively (not subjectively) as possible. Take the time to clearly identify the cause of your anger, and ask yourself if your reaction is genuinely on par with the cause.

Is flipping over the dinner table really a legitimate response and expression of anger because of poorly seasoned steak? Is screaming your fool head off at your daughter because she didn't make a goal really necessary and appropriate? Is going berserk and firing an employee because of a misunderstanding (which you very well might be the cause of) a proper course of action to deal with your loss of temper? In all cases, the answer is most likely no.

Anger is quite often very irrational. Therefore, it must be combated with logical, rational thinking and problem solving — although, admittedly, this isn't easy to do in the heat of the moment.

Take the time to think and talk things through, using open, truthful, calm communication instead of just blowing up. Reconstruct the situation, identify the root causes of the perceived injustice or threat, and strive to come to a logical, constructive, fair remedy — not just a quick act of vengeance, which ultimately solves nothing.

Another important factor in all this is to know yourself — and be honest. If you know that your passions are going to get the best of you in certain situations and settings, then do whatever you can to either avoid those things or be more prepared to deal with them in a positive manner. Have a plan of action in place. When you realize your buttons are being pushed, perhaps take a five-minute break and do something else to ease your rising temperature. Go for a walk, take a few deep breaths, do something to calm down, and keep your head on straight. Like anything else, it takes practice, work, and discipline. In fact, it takes real skill to deal appropriately with anger — and that is still the most important thing: to *deal* with it, not bury it or redirect it in unhealthy ways.

When all is said and done, though, anger can actually lead to great things. Appropriately, constructively dealing with it can bring about true justice, holiness, and freedom from sin and corruption on both the personal and communal levels. Anger is meant to spur us on to seek justice. But as I pointed out earlier, there are things that we simply have no power over, and getting insanely angry over such things is a waste of time and energy. In those times, it might be a good idea to take a minute and recite the Serenity Prayer (the longer version), which has been attributed to Reinhold Niebuhr:

> God grant me the serenity to accept the things I cannot change; courage to change the things I can; and wisdom to know the difference.

> Living one day at a time;

Enjoying one moment at a time;
Accepting hardships as the pathway to peace;
Taking, as He did, this sinful world as it is, not as I
    would have it;
Trusting that He will make all things right if I surrender
    to His Will;
That I may be reasonably happy in this life and supremely
    happy with Him forever in the next. Amen.

Much of what I've talked about here in dealing with anger in a positive manner flows from the virtue of meekness, which is the remedy for the vice of wrath. When we hear of being "meek," we often mistake it with being "weak." This is not the case; meekness is not weakness. To be *meek* means to have self-control, patience, self-discipline, and prudence. Meekness leads us to be merciful and forgiving instead of hateful and vengeful. Forgiveness heals the wounds of division and strengthens us, while vengeance only weakens us and separates us further from God and one another. To be *meek* means to bend and not break, to be flexible yet strong.

Meekness requires humility, and it's that humility that helps us realize that we are not in control: God is. Like a fisherman out at sea, we can't control the howling of the wind, the raging fury of the waters, or the disappearance of the fish that swim below; we can only control our reaction to it, and make the most of it.

God is our captain. We are in his capable hands. He has a plan, and he will bring it to completion. So the next time you find yourself "seeing red," take a moment and call to mind the words of our Lord: "Blessed are the meek, for they shall inherit the earth" (Mt 5:5). And what a great gift that inheritance is!

Chapter 7

GEAR GLUTTONY

IT WAS A DAY like any other. I went about my usual duties in a relatively calm manner. I spent the morning preparing for and celebrating Mass, visiting a few folks in the hospital, and then spent some time in the office returning phone calls and shuffling through an impressive pile of paperwork that had accumulated over the week. As lunchtime rolled around, I wrapped things up for the moment and headed out for my customary turkey sandwich on 12-grain bread, fistful of raw carrots, half-rotten apple, and gigantic glass of skim milk. On the way out of the office, I took a second to check my mailbox, as always.

I must admit that checking for mail each day has forever been one of those simple joys of life that I continually look forward to. Who knows what might be in that box? Who knows what kind of news awaits? Maybe there is a new issue of my favorite magazine in there. Perhaps I just won a million dollars! There could be a letter from a long-lost friend. Maybe there will be some nonsensical hate-mail from a fanatical, crazed lunatic — which I have to admit, I do get a kick out of. The potential for what lies in my 6-inch by 12-inch, foot-long box around the noon hour of each day is endless! I thoroughly enjoy the mystery and anticipation of the whole mail experience.

On that particular day, however, what awaited me was a new humongous outdoors catalog from a well-known store. Oh boy! My hands began to tremble and my pulse quickened as I thumbed through the thin glossy pages of outdoor supplies. *Just look at all this fantastic gear*, I exclaimed to myself. *I want all of it! I've got to have everything in this catalog! How can I go on living if*

I'm not fully equipped with all the latest gadgets and high-tech hunting and fishing goods?

Overindulging is a dangerous thing!

Immediately coming to my senses, I realized I was heading into dangerous territory, and the temptation of gear gluttony was overtaking me like a murky, stench-filled pool of quicksand. In a desperate effort to avoid the near occasion of sin, I courageously and valiantly slam-dunked the bulky catalog into the rusty, metal trash can and made myself think of something else, like ice cream, baseball cards, wafer-thin after-dinner chocolates, pancakes (I like pancakes!), or anything to get my mind off the overpowering allure of new outdoor gear.

In reality, I'm really not that uncontrollably obsessed with hunting and fishing goods. I am stretching things a bit here, but sometimes it does feel as if it gets close to that level of feverish intensity. And to be honest, there have been times in the past I have spent way too much money and accumulated far too many items that I just did not need, all because of prodigiously feasting my eyes on those mesmerizingly attractive outdoor catalogs. Such publications can be like materialistic pornography: they elicit a lustful, gluttonous desire for things one simply should not have, and one does not need.

My outdoor-gear addiction began at a young age, and there is no one to blame but myself. Oh, how I lavishly spent many a childhood afternoon glued to the pages of those same catalogs. My eyes would dance with delight as I admired the plethora of fishing rods, reels, guns, bows, camouflage clothing, camping supplies, knives, and on and on. I dreamed of the day when I would be earning more than $5 a week so that I could buy some of those things, which I was always able to thoroughly convince myself I needed.

As I admired all the new innovative outdoor products, I would imagine myself out in the wilds, fending for my life as I battled sub-zero temperatures, camping out on the frozen tundra, fishing for great white sharks, hunting fearsome polar bears, heroically saving the day — all the while utilizing and implementing all the items in those catalogs. I simply could never figure out why my parents didn't get me a new ATV or a 44-magnum pistol for Christmas. They just didn't seem to care or realize what sort of imminent adventures I'd be going on — adventures in my mind, at least!

As I've gotten older, that dreadful, yet marvelous attraction to outdoor gear hasn't subsided much. Those same catalogs from the same stores have somehow continued to follow me around everywhere I go. It's as if they are stalking me like some sort of bloodthirsty, pernicious beast just waiting to get me in its clutches and squeeze every last penny out of me! Year after year, month after month, they just keep coming — summer catalogs, winter catalogs, fall hunting specials, spring clearance sales, all that new gear, all those great deals — how can I pass them up? How can I deny them? I want to drape the whole world in camouflage, duck decoys, and fishing lures!

I heard it said once that part of the reason people buy books is because they think they are buying the time to read them. A similar phenomenon takes place in the purchasing of new out-door gear, I believe. When someone buys a new tent, he just assumes that he'll be going on a camping trip — and in fact, now he has the reasonable excuse to do so. We wouldn't be so foolish and unfettered as to buy something for no good reason, would we? Likewise, when someone buys a new fly rod, it's because she *is* going to go on that big trout-fishing trip she's been planning for so many years. With the purchase of new, rather expensive gear, one is also purchasing the justification to do whatever it takes to then actually utilize that gear. Otherwise, one (or one's spouse) will punish oneself mercilessly for wasting so much money.

Gear Mania!

In our current time, the gear craze is still going full speed ahead and gaining wallet-crushing kinetic energy every second. The items that are available to the outdoor enthusiast today are far more advanced than what was around just a decade or so ago. The advances in technology for hunting and fishing gear is truly impressive, but at the same time, rather comical in some cases.

Now don't get me wrong. Many of the things I'm about to refer to are legitimately remarkable, and I use some of these items myself. I'm certainly not bad-mouthing these things, nor am I trying to upset anyone. I'm merely pointing out the reality of what is available for this generation of outdoors men and women.

When one takes to the woods these days, he or she will probably be decked out in one of dozens and dozens of available camouflage patterns. And if one works up a sweat while hiking along in a pair of scent-free, snake-bite-resistant, waterproof, thermal-insulated boots, have no fear: the activated-charcoal-lined coveralls with quick-drying, breathable, stain-blocking, moisture-managing, bug-repelling, sound-dampening fabric will keep your human odor from wafting out upon the land and scaring away all the game (as if you were a 7-foot, 300-pound, filth-ridden Sasquatch). As an extra precaution, there's no doubt you'll be wearing some compression-fit, temperature-regulating, sweat-wicking underwear. And it, too, will be camouflaged, just in case the animals get a gander at you in your unmentionables while changing clothes or going to the timber toilet.

As any serious hunter does these days, before you even suit up to head into the great outdoors, you naturally will take a shower using scent-eliminating soap and shampoo; put on a healthy dose of scent-killing deodorant; wash your clothes in special germicidal, UV-destroying laundry detergent; and then store your duds in an odor-proof, stink-blocking container. After eating breakfast, you might use some bacteria-eliminating chewing gum to keep your disgusting dog breath from spooking the deer. As a final part of the ritual, there is a good chance you will spray yourself and all your gear down with some scent neutralizer, dab on one of various flavors of cover scent, and then, and only then, go to the woods!

While strolling through the woods, if not blazing the trails in a noisy, yet camouflaged ATV, there is no fear of getting lost or having to know how to use old-fashioned navigational tools, because you have your handy GPS unit. And don't worry about stumbling around in the dark: your Xenon/LED headlamp will keep things bright well into eternity! If a sudden chill should evoke a lung-busting cough, quickly pull out your trusty sneeze silencer to muffle that deafening blast of bad bodily air. If the silencer isn't handy and the percussion of the sneeze has stifled your hearing, just put on your hunting headset to give you supersonic hearing, while also blocking out the harmful muzzle blast.

Once you've gotten to your hunting spot — which you have been surveying all year with digital, infrared scouting cameras — you can be sure that there is plenty of wildlife around due to the self-distributing, programmable game feeders you had going in the off-season, and your efforts in planting a lush food plot, which was made easier by a vast multitude of equipment, fertilizers, and seed combinations. And if all that readily accessible, protein-packed, antler-growing deer chow doesn't lure in a big ol' buck, just hang a few scent wicks on a nearby tree and douse them with your favorite brand of hot doe in estrus to lure in that big lonely 10-pointer. As a final, added extra, set up your lifelike-motion deer decoy to close the deal.

After everything is good to go, carefully climb up into your comfy deer-lounge tree stand (with heated seat cushion, padded back and arm rests), strap yourself in with your full-body harness safety belt (in case you fall asleep while "hunting"), and get ready for some serious action! Once the sun comes up, it's good to survey the area with your binoculars and built-in digital range finder so that you can be sure of the yardage of your potential shots. Then it's time to take out your wide array of deer calls that mimic every vocalization a deer could possibly muster, many of which sound like a perfectly executed flatulent episode.

If you happen to be bowhunting, don't worry about trying to make a good shot in (legal) low-light conditions. The bright fiber-optic sight pins will glow as intense as the sun in those early morning or late evening hours. And if by chance you miss the mark, the illuminating nock on your arrow will guide you right to it. No more worrying about losing a six-dollar carbon arrow, loaded with a high-tech mechanical broadhead that cost you another five bucks. There are also no reasons to fear the loud "twang" of a released arrow, thus spooking that buck of a lifetime. The vibration- and sound-absorbing attachments on your bow will silence any possible auditory alarms. And once that deer is down, don't worry about having to use your carefully developed tracking skills: just whip out your automatic blood detector and go right to your downed animal.

All this — and much, much more — is available . . . just for hunting! I could burn up another 6 to 10 pages if I were to talk about fishing, camping, or hiking gear, but you get the point. As I mentioned, many of these things are invaluable pieces of equipment that can make the hunting experience more enjoyable, safer, and more humane regarding the actual harvesting of an animal. I'm certainly not downplaying the usefulness of such items; I'm simply illustrating how far things have progressed from the days of Daniel Boone, or of even the late great Fred Bear, for that matter. Things have come a long, long way from the ritual of putting on some old, drab clothing; lacing up a pair of mangled, grease-covered, leather work boots; lighting up a cigarette; and heading off to hunt with a clumsy, beat-up recurve bow and a few warped, splinter-ridden wooden arrows, or an ancient muzzle loader.

When considering all the gear and paraphernalia that are available today, one may think that deer or other game animals don't have a chance. As I'm always quick to point out, it is incredibly difficult to successfully harvest the likes of a wise old gobbler or trophy buck (especially with a bow) in completely natural, fair-chase settings; in areas where the animals are not semi-tame from constant human interaction; or in places that are not severely overpopulated. The animals in such natural, fair-chase settings have the clear advantage by means of their far superior senses, natural camouflage, and astonishing stealth. It is only man's superior mind and the tools he has created that give him the possibility of having the upper hand from time to time.

The End of Gear Gluttony

It's also important to keep in mind that not every outdoorsman is a gear fanatic. Many of us make it a point to *not* use many of the tools, gadgets, and high-tech items that are now available. More and more men and women these days are gravitating toward using "traditional" hunting gear to recapture the challenge, satisfaction, and discipline of doing things the hard way, as in the days of old. And as much as I'm fascinated and sometimes amused by all the latest gear, I, too, find myself using it less and less and doing things the old-fashioned way to capture the purity and reward of the hunting experience.

I also find myself doing the same thing regarding fishing, although that was not always the case. I freely admit there was a time when I was a full-blown gear glutton! When I first got seriously involved with trout fishing, I ended up acquiring every gadget and doodad that was available. I simply thought I needed, and *had* to have, everything on the market to make me the best fisherman in the land! I was a sucker for every neat, new trout-fishing implement that came along. I ended up having so much junk crammed in my fly-fishing vest that I must have weighed about 10 extra pounds. And in the long run, it only took away from the enjoyment of the trout-fishing experience.

I can vividly recall one particular outing that made me rethink the value of having so much gear. I was doing a little nighttime trout fishing for big browns on a local stream and, as usual, had my tan trout-fishing vest loaded to the hilt with a massive array of expensive, though cheaply made, plastic gear. All 32 pockets of my vest had something stuffed in them. On top of that, I had all sorts of other knickknacks attached to the outside of it. I had so much stuff on me that I would emit a rattling, clunking sound, like a pack mule stumbling across the great Western plains, as I attempted to ever-so-quietly "stalk" trout.

As evening turned into night and the lights went out, I found myself frantically fumbling around with every fish I caught. "Now where on earth are my hemostats? Which pocket did I put my flashlight in? Oh no! Was that my camera that just fell into the water? Where in the heck did I put my spilt-shot? Good gravy! Why do I have all this junk?" I needed a diagram to find where all my gear was placed. As I angrily swatted various pockets in an attempt to detect what was within, I became more and more frustrated with my predicament.

I was a walking tackle shop, but the vast majority of the items I was carrying I just didn't need. Sure, it was a neat idea to be able to do things like checking the exact water temperature, looking up insect hatches and moon phases, pumping a trout's stomach to see what it was eating, and tying a nail knot in two seconds. But all the gear that enabled me to do such things was weighing me down, getting in the way, and aggravating the heck out of me. By the time that night was over, I had simply had it!

When I got home, I violently shook and emptied all the ridiculous fishing junk out of my vest (as if I were wringing a chicken's neck!), put the things I absolutely needed in one pile, and threw the rest in a box, which I stored away . . . somewhere. The next day I went to a local military surplus store and bought a few canvas field pouches, which I then fashioned into a crude chest/back pack. I put a few simple items and the terminal tackle that I needed into the pockets, which were readily accessible, and I never looked back. This was to be my new fly-fishing apparel for years to come — and it only cost me about 15 bucks! And with that metamorphosis, my gear gluttony was destroyed.

The Vice of Gluttony and American Culture

Though I've been speaking of gluttony here as it applies to the massive, unjustified use of material things, when one considers *gluttony* in the truest sense of the word, what naturally comes to mind first is the notion of eating too much. The textbook definition of *gluttony* is the self-indulgent, excessive consumption of food and drink. We can, furthermore, add to the definition a disordered desire for bodily pleasure that is achieved through eating and drinking. The tricky and challenging thing about dealing with gluttony in this case is that it originates from a natural desire to eat.

We have to eat in order to survive. Our bodily hunger is a biological sign that we need to stoke the fire to keep ourselves going — the equivalent to the "Low Fuel" warning light in our vehicles. If we are making serious demands of our body and yet do not give it the nutrients it needs to perform and stay healthy, then it will simply break down, run out of energy, and collapse.

This natural desire for food and the act of consuming it can, however, become a source and catalyst for a multitude of problems. In 2003, the U.S. surgeon general reported that "nearly two out of every three Americans are overweight or obese," and that "one out of every eight deaths in America is caused by an illness directly related to overweight and obesity."

Here is more food for thought, taken from the same report:

- "In the year 2000, the total annual cost of obesity in the United States was $117 billion. While extra value meals may save us some change at the counter, they're costing us billions of dollars in health care and lost productivity. Physical inactivity and super-sized meals are leading to a nation of oversized people."
- "This year, more than 300,000 Americans will die from illnesses related to overweight and obesity."
- "Obesity contributes to the number-one cause of death in our nation: heart disease."
- "Excess weight has also led to an increase in the number of people suffering from Type 2 diabetes. There are at least 17 million Americans with diabetes, and another 16 million have pre-diabetes. Each year, diabetes costs America $132 billion. It can lead to eye diseases, cardiovascular problems, kidney failure, and early death."

On the other side of the coin, eating disorders such as anorexia and bulimia also affect millions of people. With anorexia, individuals do the exact opposite of gorging themselves to the point of obesity: in this case, they starve themselves. With bulimia, people binge and purge, in an attempt to remain thin or lose weight. The consequences are just as unhealthy and deadly as overeating. The extremes on either end of the spectrum lead to great danger.

So why all these problems with food? Why didn't these issues exist, to the degree we have them today, 50 years ago? Why are we getting so fat and unhealthy? There are many factors.

For one, much of our culture revolves around food, which is not necessarily a bad thing. People enjoy having a meal together. It's an opportunity to relax, spend time with family, friends, or co-workers. Food brings us together. We have food at parties, receptions, meetings, concerts, exhibitions, sporting events, on the airplane, at the movies, and everyplace in between. It seems there are places on almost every block, on nearly every street in America, where we can get a meal or a snack. We have food coming out our ears! And yet, so many still go hungry.

Much of the food we consume these days, though, is not so good for us. It is loaded with fat, cholesterol, sugar, and enough salt to melt the North Pole. No doubt it's delicious, but it's certainly not nutritious. More recently, there appears to be a growing trend to eat healthier, and there are more nutritious items available to consumers in places like fast-food restaurants — but is it too late? So many are hooked on fatty foods and snacks (especially quite a few young people) that the idea of eating tuna fish, salad, and raw fruits and vegetables simply makes their stomachs turn and their jaws lock shut in revolt!

The simple reality is that there is pleasure in filling one's gullet by eating food that tastes good — and therein lies another problem. When we become conditioned to only eat food that tastes good, it becomes burdensome to consume food that is not so good tasting, even though it is nutritionally good and vitally needed for overall health. Thus, the dinner table is surrounded by chubby, whining, ungrateful mouths that long for a 10,000-calorie, belly-bombing bacon cheeseburger, along with a double-chin chocolate cake, and a vanilla fatso-deluxe shake to wash it all down, instead of a spinach salad and some fat-free, hard-earned, venison tenderloin.

Loss of Control

This uncontrollable desire for pleasurable foods can lead not only to being overweight or obese but also to food addiction. Just as some people can develop an uncontrollable craving for nicotine, alcohol, drugs, or sex, so there are others in our world who have developed a disordered desire for food. There are many different reasons for this. For some, their addiction is born out of trying to cope with difficult situations in their lives. There are many things in their daily experiences that make them feel bad, such as abuse, neglect, loneliness, feelings of inadequacy or worthlessness, lack of control, stress, and depression. In such cases, food is one of the few things that *makes* them feel good; hence, it becomes a crutch to lean on and a cherished oasis in times of distress. As with any addiction, it is not just a matter of having "no will power." There are many psychological factors to be considered.

Another culprit that can certainly play a part in our national weight gain is the general lack of physical activity and the sedentary lifestyle that so many live. Millions of kids are "glued" to the computer or spend all day playing video games while eating pants-popping garbage instead of going outside to play or doing something that involves exercise. Millions of adults have office jobs and after work simply don't have the time, or take the time, to hit the gym for an hour or so a few times a week before going home to take care of family or home needs.

Another contributing factor to eating disorders comes from the corporate body-image gurus of our day who design, manufacture, and sell to young women, and teens in general, the idea that unless they weigh 60 pounds and we can see their hip bones, they are simply unacceptable and undesirable. Thus, healthy adolescents (and people of all ages, really) who naturally have some meat on their bones will spend hours researching the latest diets, downing diet pills, starving themselves, consulting cosmetic surgeons, and doing anything they can to desperately rid themselves of every trace of fat on their bodies in order to gain the approval of others, to live up to the images that have quite literally been sold to them, and to mistakenly believe they can win the great trophy of self-worth.

With regard to actual gluttony, some become enslaved by this vice because they choose to, and others do so because of factors that perhaps originally had nothing to do with food. Whatever the case may be, the bottom line is that a glutton desires pleasure and achieves that pleasure by consuming way too much, by becoming extremely, dangerously self-indulgent. While it certainly applies to food and drink, it can apply to virtually anything that we consume or *use* to give us pleasure.

Just as the bodily result of food gluttony is gaining weight and putting one's health at risk, so the underlying end result for any kind of gluttony is a lack of lasting satisfaction; an undisciplined, unbalanced, and unattainable desire for disordered pleasure; and an overdriven, uncontrollable appetite. Gluttons will always want more — though they certainly do not need more — and they cannot stop that desire for more. It rules their lives. For gluttons, "their God is the belly" (Phil 3:19).

The ability to control our appetites says a lot about us as a whole. It is often a reflection of the state of one's soul. If one cannot control the desire for pleasurable foods and maintain balance, there most likely will be similar imbalances in other areas of one's life, which manifest themselves in things such as the inability to control one's gossiping tongue, bad temper, lustful thoughts, sexual desires, and envious heart. When our appetites take control of our lives, we are in big trouble. We truly become slaves. We become chained, owned, and ordered by a master who will never be satisfied, and who couldn't care less how his unachievable directives beat us down and destroy us, day in and day out.

When one is enslaved to pleasure by means of consumption, the stimuli to achieve that pleasure increases constantly. What it took to acquire temporary satisfaction one day will increase the next. For the glutton, the eating of one bowl of ice cream eventually turns into the devouring of an entire quart. The contentment of drinking a glass of wine after a long day at work turns into the chugging of the entire bottle. The pleasure of buying and using a new fishing lure turns into the uncontrollable need to buy everything in the store. When we lose control, we lose ourselves.

The Power of Temperance and Moderation

How does one gain control? How does one break those chains and begin to regain freedom? With temperance, with self-control, by exercising the will, and by implementing discipline in one's life. The virtue of temperance is the habit of moderation. It is the governing and mastering of one's appetites. It's the ability to conquer one's urges and desires for that which is sinfully excessive.

Scripture has a lot to say about the virtue of temperance and moderation. In Sirach, we read:

> Do not follow your inclination and strength. . . .
> My son, test your soul while you live;
>   see what is bad for it and do not give it that.
> For not everything is good for every one,
>   and not every person enjoys everything.
> Do not have an insatiable appetite for any luxury,
>   and do not give yourself up to food;
> for overeating brings sickness,
>   and gluttony leads to nausea.
> Many have died of gluttony,
>   but he who is careful to avoid it prolongs his life.
>   (Sir 5:2; 37:27-31)

Sirach also advises us, "Do not follow your base desires, / but restrain your appetites. / If you allow your soul to take pleasure

in base desire, / it will make you the laughingstock of your ene-
mies" (Sir 18:30-31). St. Paul also gives us good counsel in his
letter to Titus, as he instructs everyone to "renounce irreligion
and worldly passions, and to live sober, upright, and godly lives
in this world" (Titus 2:12).

Just as one gets in the habit of losing control, indulging
excesses, and living an intemperate life, so one needs to reverse
the process and get in the habit of getting control and exercising discipline and temperance. This is easier said than done, of
course, but we have been given all the tools we need to build up
virtue and pulverize vice in our lives. One of the greatest tools
God has given us to do this with is our will. As I mentioned earlier, many claim to have "no will power" over certain things, and
that very well may be true. But that is most likely because they
have not exercised their *power of the will*. Just like any muscle of
the body, if the will is not exercised, strengthened, and built up,
it will atrophy and become emaciated, weak, and worthless —
and it will fail you when you need it most.

When we look at the vices and bad habits of our lives, they
didn't just happen overnight. It was a steady process of indulging ourselves and giving in to temptation, a little at a time, and
becoming just a bit more lax than the previous day. It's a process
of letting down our guard slightly further every time we're faced
with those strong, self-indulgent desires. As time goes on, we
simply have no guard left, and we just throw up our hands in
defeat, then surrender and say, "What's the use? I can't fight it!
I give up!" And we then jump right into the consuming fire of
vice. The longer that self-defeating mind-set goes unchecked,
unchallenged, and uncorrected, the more our habit of sinfulness
and vice grows, and the weaker and more enslaved we become.

Exercise the Will
That process of slowly breaking down and succumbing to temptation must therefore be reversed. And the only way to do that

is to actively exercise the will. Sure, it's hard to do at first. Just like someone who hasn't done a sit-up, push-up, or run a mile in years, that first effort feels as though it's going to kill him or her. The muscles will twitch and shake awkwardly as the fibers try to efficiently regroup and contract with some degree of force. The heart rate will race with the sudden rush of blood that's being pumped into places that it hasn't been in years. The lungs will burn, heave, and gasp, desperately trying to acquire the necessary oxygen to fuel this strange new demand that is being made on the body.

It's not easy getting back in shape. In fact, it's downright torturous! But we simply *must be* disciplined to keep at it a little at a time. And the more we do it, the easier it gets. It becomes self-motivating, and before long, we are back up to speed, on track, and in control of the things in life that we can and should be in control of. But don't forget: God has the ultimate control!

In regard to exercising the will, the same principles apply. We simply have to make the conscious decision to use it, and then use it a little more every day. As I'm always quick to mention, runners or other athletes only make improvements by *willing themselves* to run that extra quarter mile or lifting that extra 10 pounds. Proper training, a balanced diet, adequate rest, and all the other necessary factors are important, of course. But when it's all said and done, in the heat of the battle, it comes down to making the decision to *do it!* To go that extra step, *no matter what!*

In exercising the will, we again have to simply decide to make those consistent, small improvements; to be a little more patient than we were yesterday; to be a little more temperate; to be a little more prudent, etc. We have to take those small steps in the right direction each day — and when we fall flat on our face, we have to make the conscious decision to get back up.

As the old saying goes, the longer you stay down when the horse throws you off, the harder it'll be to get back on and ride. Sure, there are setbacks and times when we seem to be going downhill again, but we must persevere! That's why the Lord gives us a lifetime to get our act together. Our lives and our sanctity are works in progress.

Overcoming Addiction

Now, even though all this talk of exercising the will might sound great, there is still the reality of true addiction setting in and a vice or bad habit becoming seemingly unbreakable. Oftentimes we like to use the excuse that we are "addicted" to something, when in reality we are not: we're just plain lazy and don't want to put forth the effort to improve. But when true, genuine addiction takes over, the will is of no avail. After we've honestly put forth 100 percent, maximum effort, and have persevered as much as humanly possible over a significant period of time to overcome an issue we're struggling with, and just cannot break the cycle, it's then that we need to call upon and rely on higher powers.

One of the most successful (if not *the* most successful) programs for overcoming addiction is the 12-step program of Alcoholics Anonymous, which was originally developed in the late 1930s by Bill Wilson and Dr. Bob Smith. These 12 steps have been applied to addiction-recovery programs for anything you could possibly think of, and they essentially revolve around this calling and relying upon a higher power. The 12 steps, which are fairly self-explanatory, are as follows:

1. We admitted we were powerless over alcohol [or whatever else one is addicted to] — that our lives had become unmanageable.
2. Came to believe that a Power greater than ourselves could restore us to sanity.
3. Made a decision to turn our will and our lives over to the care of God as we understood Him.
4. Made a searching and fearless moral inventory of ourselves.

5. Admitted to God, to ourselves, and to another human being the exact nature of our wrongs.

6. Were entirely ready to have God remove all these defects of character.

7. Humbly asked Him to remove our shortcomings.

8. Made a list of all persons we had harmed, and became willing to make amends to them all.

9. Made direct amends to such people wherever possible, except when to do so would injure them or others.

10. Continued to take personal inventory and when we were wrong promptly admitted it.

11. Sought through prayer and meditation to improve our conscious contact with God as we understood Him, praying only for knowledge of His will for us and the power to carry that out.

12. Having had a spiritual awakening as the result of these steps, we tried to carry this message to alcoholics [or addicts], and to practice these principles in all our affairs. (*Alcoholics Anonymous*, Fourth Edition, 2001)

Here, too, it's not easy to take that first step in getting help or to actually admit that one is hopelessly addicted to something. In such cases, it is often painfully obvious to everyone else except the addict. Denial is a powerful thing. And so, the necessary ingredient in all cases is the grace of God. I've discussed grace previously, but in case you've forgotten, it is a free and undeserved gift that God gives to us so that we may live out the life he has called us to, which is a good, healthy, and holy life. Grace is the life of God within us, and it draws us into a deeper friendship and relationship with him. It sanctifies us. It helps us to develop in the ways of virtue and leave behind the ways of vice. Grace assists us in transforming our will, to be in accordance with God's will.

We acquire grace in many ways, but ultimately it's by being in union and communion with the Lord. We receive grace by living out our faith and constantly growing closer to him. We have to be able to admit that while we can accomplish astonishing things, and can will ourselves to the moon, we still are human beings, who are breakable, sinful, weak, and in need of life, love, and truth. As we've already seen, it's only God who can give us these things. And so it's in coming to know, love, and serve God, and by staying in his good graces, that we are healed of our brokenness, of our uncontrollable desires, and of all the things that rob us of life and freedom. If there is one thing we should be gluttons for, it's the love, mercy, and grace of God. We can never have too much of it, and he is always there waiting to fill our plate back up. So dig in, my friend!

Chapter 8

ELK LUST

ON DECEMBER 9, 2006, my life as a bowhunter and outdoorsman forever changed. On that day, I received a letter from a man named Bob Reineke, who lives with his wife, Cathy, in north-central Idaho. In his letter, Bob gave me some background information on himself and kindly expressed his appreciation for my first book, *Hunting for God, Fishing for the Lord*. He also casually, but sincerely, offered me an invitation to come up to Idaho someday and fish for trout and smallmouth, or to hunt for elk, bear, turkey, and whitetails. Probably thinking I wouldn't respond or take him seriously, he included some references, such as the name and phone number of his pastor, to perhaps verify that his offer and personal credibility were verifiable. After all, who would blindly head to north-central Idaho to meet up with a total stranger, to go on a wild outdoor adventure, all on account of a simple written invitation?

Upon my initial reading of Bob's letter, two words lit up like the Milky Way in the vast Northwestern summer skies: "hunt" and "elk"! It had been my lifelong dream to head west and bowhunt for elk. It is something I never imagined I'd be able to do — at least not for a long, long time, if ever. The thought of stalking through the rugged, wild, untamed lands of the Northwest with bow in hand, in pursuit of a huge, rather intimidating, majestic, bugling beast, was simply too much for me to fathom. *It'll just never happen*, I would always tell myself with a sigh of sadness.

As I read over Bob's letter a second time, I began to realize that this was, in fact, the real deal. Now, let me tell you, I have the uncanny ability to sniff out a "nut" from a mile away. But I could easily recognize by the professionalism in Bob's writing and the very structure of the letter that he was not some crazed, hateful stalker, driven by a deep-seated vendetta, out to lure me into some methodically planned-out trap to bring about my demise in the most barbaric and medieval fashion one could possibly conjure!

I replied to Bob, thanking him for his letter and his kind words about the book. I also mentioned that if he was serious, and if it wouldn't be any burden on him or his wife, I'd be more than interested in coming up for a hunt.

And so it began! The hunt of a lifetime, and more importantly, a newfound friendship was about to be forged.

Over the next several months, Bob and I stayed in touch by e-mail and prepared for the hunt. Because Bob has family that lives here in the St. Louis area, I was eventually able to visit with Cathy and him when they came to town for a visit. It was a real joy to finally meet them in person, to get to know them better, and to talk about our upcoming hunt in mid-September.

As the weeks went by, leading up to the big trip out west, I still couldn't believe it was for real. For a guy who can't sleep for weeks because he gets so excited about hunting and fishing trips, I simply wasn't on fire yet. Again, I literally could not believe it was going to happen; it was beyond my ability to intellectually digest the reality of it.

Just a few weeks before the trip, I had another big surprise. One day as I was checking my e-mail, I got a totally out-of-the-blue message from elk-hunting expert and author Jay Houston. Jay had recently moved from Colorado to the St. Louis area. Jay and I got together for lunch, exchanged books, and had a great time visiting. Though we mostly talked about the Lord, faith, and ministry, we also, of course, talked about hunting, and Jay gave me some valuable pointers. If you need some good, solid, reliable information on elk hunting, check out Jay's books or visit him online at *www.ElkCamp.com*.

At last, the day finally arrived. Having, thankfully, decided to fly instead of drive to Idaho (which actually came out much cheaper in the long run), I was dropped off at Lambert Airport by my parents. As I walked through the terminal, I realized that I had in my possession a plane ticket to Idaho, an elk tag, and my bow — three things I never in my wildest dreams thought I'd have all at once! The reality was slowly beginning to set in ... but not much ... I still just couldn't believe it!

As I sat in my cramped plane seat and peered out the window at the jagged, mountainous terrain of the Western landscape below, I called to mind the fact that I was genuinely journeying in the footsteps of Lewis and Clark, from St. Charles, Missouri, to Orofino, Idaho. Because my childhood stomping grounds were actually located on the exact spot of the Lewis and Clark rendezvous in 1804, I found it very fitting to be traveling (although not the exact route) in their same direction. That pioneer spirit has always been in my blood!

About an hour before the plane touched down, I found myself in prayerful reflection. I thanked the Lord for this incredible blessing, and for the opportunity to (even possibly) fulfill my lifelong dream. I asked God to keep Bob and me safe and sound, to sanctify our time in his wonderful creation — and if it was his will, to help us fill our elk tags! But I have to tell you that, yet again, even though I was totally prepared for the hunt (physically, mentally, and spiritually); even though I'd honed my archery skills to a newfound level of perfection; and even though I'd even made several trips to a local wildlife park to get up close to tame elk in order to condition my nerves for a possible close encounter with "real" wild elk, I still had zero expectations for filling my tag. Not that I didn't want it to happen, and not that I wouldn't put forth 1,000,000 percent effort to make it happen (God willing), but I still just couldn't even grasp the actuality of it being a possibility. I expected to explore some incredibly beautiful land and waters; to have a great time of fellowship with

Bob; and to see a fair amount of wildlife and perhaps have a few close encounters with some elk. But the idea of actually harvesting an elk with my bow was just far too good to be true.

In one sense, though, that zero expectation was the perfect mind-set. Knowing full well that unfulfilled expectations are often the root of interior self-destruction, my forced lowering of *all* expectation for a successful hunt kept me calm, collected, focused, and prepared for anything. I had nowhere to go but up — and as I found out during the hunt, there would be lots of "going up" in the next week!

Hunting the Great Wapiti

At last, after a few hours in the sky — which sure beat two days of nonstop driving — the plane touched down at the small airport of Lewiston, Idaho, where Bob and Cathy were waiting to pick me up. After saying hello and "shooting the bull" (something we hoped to do later in the week with an arrow!), I hopped into their sizable, rugged truck, and we headed to their home near Orofino, to visit for the day and get things prepared for the beginning of our weeklong adventure, set to begin the next morning.

After a lovely afternoon, taking in the beauty of the area and the serenity of their homestead, Bob, Cathy, and me, along with their friends Monty and Robbin, spent the evening sharing a delicious meal of grilled elk steaks and hearty homegrown vegetables. (Cathy is quite the gardener and cook!) As the enchanted evening came to a close, a family of deer fed in the lush field right outside the window of the dining room — a fitting end to a wonderful, but long, day of travel.

When morning came, Bob and I loaded up the dusty truck and began the two-hour drive to where we'd launch his noble cedar canoe up the North Fork Clearwater River, en route to our hunt area, nestled in the Clearwater Mountains. It felt as though we were, in fact, Lewis and Clark, as our standard-sized canoe was loaded with so much gear and provisions that I thought we'd sink for sure! Thankfully, Bob had two small stabilizing pontoons on both sides of the canoe to keep us securely afloat.

Even though we didn't have to do much paddling, the small, two-horsepower outboard engine attached to the back of our finely crafted vessel didn't exactly speed us along the seven-mile stretch we had to travel to get to our primitive campsite way in the backcountry. It was another couple of hours to get to our destination. But I was certainly in no hurry, and I suspect Bob was not, either. The peace and tranquility of taking in the boundless expanses of beautiful north-central Idaho, from a slow-moving canoe, was a captivating, meditative, prayerful journey. It gave me the opportunity to once again get in my daily solid hour of undisturbed prayer.

Along the way, we saw a big black bear sneaking along, high up on a ridge top. We watched osprey as well as bald and golden eagles hovering in the heavens and diving down to feed on the spawning Kokanee salmon. And we spotted many whitetail deer, chewing and munching on the green browse along the steep riverbank. Much to my surprise, there were also a few great blue herons flying around, stalking the riverbanks for fish.

(I've always considered the great blue heron my outdoors mascot. Ever since I was a kid, no matter where I was, there was always one present when I was in the outdoors — always! It was a good omen. Though the otherwise blue skies were filled with a bit of a smoke-filled haze from the wildfires that summer, it was still a stunning scene to behold.)

After quickly setting up the rest of camp and getting our gear in order, Bob and I headed out for an evening hunt, though mainly a scouting expedition. It didn't take long for me to realize all the more that Bob is a very serious, exceptionally intelligent, razor-sharp outdoorsman and hunter. He is a man of great forethought, as well as kind consideration. It was obvious, too, that he is a faith-filled, spiritual individual who relishes and appreciates God's gifts as much as I do — and makes no bones about expressing it.

At close to 60 years old and retired, Bob often referred to himself as an "old man" — but let me tell you, that "old man" is in better shape than most men half his age. Heck, at times it was difficult for me to keep up with him! It was a great joy, and a really refreshing privilege, to hunt with someone who did things the old-fashioned way, the highly productive and deeply satisfying way, and that is ... *the hard way!*

Part of Bob's strategy was for us to hunt an area where the noisy 200-horsepower jetboat, ATV-riding, four-by-four monster truck, high-tech, gear-junkie hunters couldn't, or wouldn't, get to. They would likely be at higher elevations in other areas, making all kinds of noise, and pushing the elk back down to us, in the more inaccessible areas. Now, I'll be the first to admit that ATVs and all those other modes of transportation and tools can be of great value, especially out in the wilds of miles and miles of public land. They can certainly make life much easier and aid tremendously with the backbreaking chores that come along with such exhausting pursuits as big game hunting. *But*, quite often, those things simply become the expensive attachments and overpriced toys of gear-glutton hunters who are just plain lazy, out of shape, ill-prepared, and dangerously hyped-up to fill a tag as quickly and easily as humanly possible.

Bob and I had a good laugh one evening when a big boatload of such fellows did actually venture into our area, noisily speeding up the river at full throttle, on the verge of bottoming out in the shallow, rocky water, all the while peering through raised binoculars, attempting to "scout" the surrounding land for elk. Upon seeing us quietly sitting along the bank in a little ol' canoe, they stopped and yelled, "Hey! Did you guys see any elk? Where are they? Where are they?"

As their noise pollution echoed through the mountains and hills, I'm sure every living creature around had a good laugh at their "stealthy" approach to scouting as well. It was a humorous but rude intrusion on the peace and tranquility of the evening. But then again, it was public land. They had a right to be there as much as we did, and that kind of thing will happen from time to time. Thankfully, it was the only such unwelcome encounter with the great two-legged North American Jackass! (I guess I shouldn't call people that. I say it jokingly — but I just can't help it!)

Anyhow, getting back to the first evening of the hunt, Bob and I followed some game trails up, up, up the hills and mountains. We found some exceptionally fresh "sign" — still "steaming," in fact, if you know what I mean! As we ventured for miles, way up some more, we saw many huge antler rubs on tattered, beat-up trees. And we saw the telltale signs of bears and cougars, who, along with wolves, inhabit those parts in great numbers — which can make a guy from the Midwest look over his shoulder a few more times than usual!

Though it was cold, in the 30s, during the late evenings, nights, and early mornings, the afternoons were downright hot, getting into the high 80s and even the low 90s! Despite the cooler, extremely thick, dense, inhospitable woods — which were littered everywhere with massive dead-fallen trees — I still worked up one heck of a sweat on that first outing. And though we didn't see or hear any elk, it was an eye-opening introduction to the area we'd be hunting and living in for the next six days.

It was also a stern reality check, because I now fully understood what I'd been reading for so many years: namely, that elk hunting is tough, and exceptionally physically demanding, hard work! It is nothing at all like kicking back in a cozy tree stand, fairly relaxed, on the edge of a food plot, crop field, or oak tree at your local 40-acre whitetail deer spread (which I'm certainly not criticizing). Let me tell you something, folks: If you are not willing to push yourself to the max, to be very uncomfortable,

and to work your butt off, then don't bother bowhunting elk —
at least not on real, wild, public land.

As our first evening expedition came to a close, we trekked
back to the canoe and headed downstream to camp. The sound
of the sleek wooden paddles lapping in the cool, clear water
made me even thirstier, as we were close to calling it a day. Back
at camp, we re-stoked our bodily furnaces on some simple but
nourishing food, and hit the sack. (I have to tell you, it was great
to hunt with a guy who appreciates the value of a good peanut
butter sandwich!)

As the smoky, silken sun began to lose its blinding blaze and
rapidly descend behind a buttress of conifers, I was so tired from
the previous day's travel and the afternoon hiking that I fell right
to sleep in my rather tight, miserably cumbersome, sleeping bag.
The stillness of the night, the soft chirping of crickets, and the
cool river-bottom air knocked me right out!

At 4 o'clock the next morning, the trusty alarm on my cheap
digital watch (I'm the king of cheap digital watches) woke me
from my deep, therapeutic slumber. As I pried myself out of the
python-death-grip of my mummy-style sleeping bag, the cold
morning temperature woke me up fast. It was freezing! I quickly
put on all my hunting clothes to warm up and get my blood
flowing. That was my fastest effort to get moving in the morning in a long time! After a relatively quick breakfast consisting
of a nice, ripe banana, dry cereal and powdered milk, and strong,
camp coffee, we got geared up and headed upstream in the canoe
to our hunt zone.

As part of my attempt to keep my human odor covered
up during the hunt, I attached some cow elk urine cover scent
wafers to myself. Believe me, those things smell far, far worse
than they sound! Poor Bob was downwind in the back of the
canoe, turning green, and he gently asked me to wait until we
got into the woods before I put those things on next time. Of
course, it wasn't exactly great to be on the trail-end of the elk-

urine-soaked rag he had on his backpack all day, either! I sure hope the elk appreciated it!

After landing the canoe in the placid morning twilight, we began our hunt. Once again it was up, up, and away as we slowly, quietly as possible, moved through the mountains and the hills, constantly aware of the wind direction so as not to be smelled and busted by any unseen elk. Just like the evening before, we found a fair amount of extremely fresh sign, but it seemed the elk were just one step ahead of us.

Around 8:15, after covering a few miles already, we finally heard a bull bugle in the distance! Wow! It was the first time I'd heard that in the wild. There is just nothing on earth like the sound of a bull elk screaming, roaring, bellowing, and letting loose with his signature bugle. Even from far away, it makes the hair stand up on the back of one's neck with excitement and exhilaration!

We kept walking in the direction of the bull, and eventually we jumped a few bedded-down elk. I only saw one cow through the thick timber, but the woods were filled with the sounds of trees snapping and dirt flying! It was as though several high-speed bulldozers were taking off up the hill, obliterating everything in their path! We stayed still for a few minutes and did some soft cow calling. Sure enough, the cows started calling back to us. (It was similar to what happens when a flock of turkeys, which has been broken up, is trying to come back together.)

The cows were sounding off all around us, trying to regroup, and amidst the cow "mews" there were a few bugles from the local bull. It sounded as though they were responding to Bob's soft calling, so we set up in preparation for a shot. My blood began to flow faster and my heart was doing double time as the "thud" of the heavy footsteps got closer. But then, they just seemed to disappear. It never ceased to amaze me that week how such gigantic, quarter-ton (or bigger) animals could move so fast — and could see, smell, and hear so well — and virtually vanish into thin air in the blink of an eye! Outstanding!

An hour or two later, as the morning progressed, we finally heard a couple more bugles. They were fairly close, and there seemed to be two different bulls. Once again we tried to move in on them and get their attention, but they just weren't having any of it. They stayed up higher on the mountain and wouldn't come back down to us. We could have used a few noisy ATV guys that day! Around 10 o'clock in the morning, it was getting very warm, and the elk were bedded down and done for the day, so we went back to camp, regrouped, and did a little fishing and some glassing/scouting in the evening.

The "Miracle Bull"

Day three began much like the first: up at 4 o'clock, frozen to death, warmed up quickly, prayed, ate, went to the latrine, hit the river. After landing the canoe and putting the rest of our hunting gear on (gloves, face masks, and cow elk urine "stink wafers," as we called them) we climbed up the steep, muddy yet rocky, riverbank and prepared to enter the timber, on the trail of some especially fresh tracks we found. Right before entering the woods, Bob gave a quiet, subtle cow call, "Meeeew," as if to say in elk talk, "Where are you, elky-elk? Don't leave me behind — especially not you, Mr. Big Bad Bull. Can't you hear that I'm a lovely, lonely cow just waiting to be a part of your fall harem?" (By the way, the bulls do, in fact, gather up actual harems of cows during the rut [breeding season], even though it is the cow who decides which bull she'll allow to breed her.)

After just that one soft call, I immediately heard a frenzied bugle cut through the cold, early morning air in the far-off distance somewhere. I took a quick look around, and way down on the far end of the riverbank, up on a steep, rocky hill, on the other side of a small ridge, I noticed what looked like a brown dot, about 300-400 yards away, moving around. Bob did another call, and sure enough, another passionate bugle came right back! I excitedly whispered to Bob, "Good gravy! That's an elk down there . . . a bull!" We both looked back down the line, and now that "brown dot" was getting bigger and moving fast in our direction.

The bull continued to bugle, and let loose that blood-curdling primal scream, as he came racing toward us in high gear! An elk can cover 100 yards in a matter of seconds, so Bob and I quickly crouched down low and scampered across the rocky terrain to gain some ground and get into position. There was just one little ridge keeping us out of the bull's sight as we made our move. After closing the distance as much as possible, we set up in some sparse brush to try to conceal ourselves as best we could. Though the woods were thick as could be, out on the high riverbanks and muddy meadow areas there was virtually no cover at all, except for some decrepit, washed-out, old stumps, some scattered dead trees, and a few thigh-high patches of grass scattered about here and there.

Still going berserk with his crazed vocalizations, the bull was just moments away from popping over the ridge and coming into view. There was a small, though fairly deep gully a ways out in front of us. At the last moment, Bob mentioned he didn't think the bull would cross it, and so he quickly suggested that I hurry up and get over in front of it. With lightning speed and careful stealth I did so — but now, I really had no cover. The biggest thing for me to use to break up my outline and conceal myself was a *knee*-high patch of grass! Thus, with my heart pounding and adrenaline pumping as never before, I knelt down and hunkered in as far as I could in that bit of greenery.

With Bob now a ways behind me, again doing seductive cow calling (an ideal setup for tag-teaming elk), the bull suddenly emerged from up over the ridge top, 30 yards in front of me. He looked like the stag from the Hartford Insurance logo!

It was unbelievable, nerve-racking, a bit frightening, and breathtakingly beautiful beyond words to see that massive, hulking, red-eyed beast look to the heavens with his gargantuan, white-tipped, six-by-six rack in the skyline as he bugled and roared his head off, right in front of me. It was deafening! I thought I would mess my drawers! It sounded like the end of the world! But he was quartering to me, and I didn't have a good shot. Then he got nervous and aggravated when he didn't see the cow he thought he had heard and began to leave.

Finally, Bob gave one more provocative cow call as if to say in wapiti (elk), "Now, you're not leaving me are you, big boy? Hmmm? Wink . . . wink!" That did it! Suddenly, the bull whipped around and came in broadside, giving me a perfect 25-yard-shot opportunity. I thought for sure he would pick me off and see me when I drew the bow, but it was now or never. The earth stood still as I nestled down farther in that patch of tall grass. Time and space froze as I knelt there on the steep rugged terrain of the North Fork Clearwater River at 6:05 a.m., September 13, 2007, just three days before my 34th birthday.

For the next few seconds, I seemed to truly be in another dimension. I remember thinking to myself as I tried to ward off an adrenaline-induced heart attack: *My Lord! I didn't even expect to see a bull elk . . . and now this! This guy is huge! This is far beyond my wildest dreams and expectations. If I could have written a fantasy script for this hunt, it wouldn't have ever been this good!*

At last, I went for it and drew back my bow as steadily and slowly as I could, with absolutely no excessive movement whatsoever, just as I practice with every shot I take year-round. And finally, as I took careful aim and gently touched off the arrow, I could literally see the feathers spin and hear the wind coming off the arrow like helicopter blades in slow motion, as it headed for the bull, exactly to the spot I was focusing on.

Though I didn't actually see the arrow hit (I seemed to have temporarily blacked out or something), I heard what sounded like a two-by-four snapping in half, and I saw the bull run up the mountain into the thick woods. Seconds later I heard a loud crash! I thought I had either made a good hit and he was done (it doesn't take long for a well-placed arrow to do the job), or that I missed and he was just making lots of noise during his escape.

When the bull was out of sight, I got up, took a huge breath of relief, and waited for Bob to come over. He had a smile on his face and said, "You must have heard my prayer. I was praying to God that you'd release your arrow when he was there, broadside. When I heard it hit, I knew you did! You probably wouldn't get that chance again. Congratulations! And hey, if you don't mind, you can take off that stink wafer now!" So, with violently trembling hands, I fumbled around and put the awful-smelling plastic disk back in its airtight container, while trying to regain some semblance of composure.

Though Bob seemed fairly confident of a hit, as did I, I didn't want to jump the gun and start celebrating yet. Neither of us was totally sure as to where the arrow went, nor whether that loud crash was the bull going down for the count or just escaping through the woods. After settling my nerves for about 30 minutes, Bob and I began looking for sign at the spot where the bull stood when apparently, hopefully, hit — but we didn't see any blood anywhere. As we examined the immediate area, I saw the back end of my arrow sticking out of a clump of grass . . . and there was no blood on the feathers!

My heart sank to the bottom of the sea. "Oh no! I missed!" All the bad shots I've ever made (which aren't too many, thankfully) flashed before my eyes. As I bent over and picked up my arrow, though, I quickly noticed that the other half of it was gone and nowhere to be found. It was in the bull! He simply broke it off after the impact! It was a good sign.

Still with great care, though, we began slowly and ever so cautiously looking for the beginning of a blood trail. After several minutes, I finally found just a slight smudge of blood on a blade of grass at the entrance to the dense forest. "I've got blood!" I exclaimed to Bob. We marked the spot and began looking for the next. A few yards up the trail, I found just another small drop. He didn't seem to be bleeding badly at all. Not good! Was it a low hit, a high hit, or a gut shot? Things still didn't look very promising. For the next hour, we step-by-inching-step analyzed virtually every leaf, every blade of grass, every twig, and everything in or around the area of the apparent trail the bull followed up the hill.

I had never prayed with so much feverish intensity (while hunting) in all my life. I invoked the powers of heaven along that trail like never before! As the blood trail became even more sparse, I thought I would throw up from the anxiety and stomach-churning nervousness that I was experiencing on that tracking job. It felt as if I'd just consumed a two-liter bottle of ipecac and it was about to take effect!

As I was bent over looking for the spoor (the track), my tongue hung out of my mouth like a sick dog and became salty as my head began to pound from the blood flowing fast into my skull. Finally, as I stood up straight to regain my composure and clear my cranium, I saw him! There he was, just another 30 yards up the hill. He was down, propped up against a demolished tree.

"Bob!" I shouted. "There he is!" Bob advised me to ever so carefully go up around him to confirm that he was, in fact, expired and would not charge and make human shish kebabs out of us that morning.

I eased up on that gigantic, 700-pound beast and discovered he was, in fact, done. Upon later examination, we found out that it was, as I thought, a lung shot (very quick and fatal); but since there was no arrow penetration out the other side, he bled internally for the most part and did not leave a good blood trail. I knelt down in front of the huge bull elk, put my hands on his behemoth shoulders, and spent a few moments now thanking God like never before.

I thought I would cry. In fact, I may have. But the joy was certainly not all mine. This harvest and hunt was a tag-team effort. It was "our" bull. Without Bob's calling skills, elk knowledge, and, of course, his invitation to hunt in the first place, this never would have happened. After sharing the victory with Bob and spending several minutes in prayerful appreciation of this magnificent animal, we took some pictures and then got to work.

Father Joe and the mighty bull elk in the wilds of Idaho

Let me tell you something, my friends: Packing a 700-pound animal (in quarters weighing up to 90 pounds) out of the mountains, several hundred yards along the steep, rough riverbanks, and seven miles back to our launch point in a little canoe, with just one other guy, was like running a marathon and participating in the World's Strongest Man competition all in one day! Brutal!

After cooling and washing the meat in some cold mountain creek water, Bob and I had to make several trips to haul it all out. It was agonizing, backbreaking work! I offered up the pain and anguish as a prayer and sacrifice ("redemptive suffering" is what we Catholics call it) for those members of my parish back home who were sick and dealing with illnesses. As Archbishop Fulton Sheen used to say, "Don't waste your pain!"

It was midnight when we finally wrapped things up. And because there were no meat lockers available that evening, we put the quarters in huge coolers with ice and left them outside in the chilly Idaho air overnight at Bob and Cathy's home. The next morning we found a place to take care of the meat, and then headed back to the woods for an elk for Bob.

For the remaining days of the hunt, I was badly beaten down. I was exhausted, but still having an awesome time! I kept pushing myself on, doing all I could to help close the deal for Bob over the next few days. Although we had a few close encounters — very close encounters, in fact — and spotted a true monster whitetail buck (whom we nicknamed "Idaho Man"), we just couldn't get another bull or bring a good cow in close enough.

The elk activity continued as it had for the earlier part of the week, with hardly any bugling or movement, except for late evening and very early morning. The only other bugling we heard was at 2 a.m. one night when two bulls were sounding off back and forth across the river for over an hour, around our campsite.

As the week came to a close, the elk we had harvested became known as the "Miracle Bull." It was as if God himself had reached down from heaven and placed that big wapiti right there on the riverbank that morning. Everything just seemed to work with textbook perfection.

It was far beyond mere "good luck." Obviously, there was skill involved in calling, stalking, setting up, tracking, and making the shot on that elk. But there was also an overriding feeling that our successful hunt that morning was truly a gift from God. It was simply meant to be, and for that I'm forever grateful. (To make the victory even sweeter, I found out a couple of months later that the Miracle Bull had made it into the *Pope & Young* archery record book. My first elk bowhunt and my first P&Y record! What are the chances of that?)

Father Joe, Bob Reineke, and the sofa-sized "Miracle Bull"

On the last day of the hunt, we broke camp, made two trips up and down the river to pack everything back to the truck, and finally headed to Orofino. The next morning I got on a plane in Lewiston at 6:30 and came home. I was almost 15 pounds lighter and still more than a bit worn out, but flowing through my veins, and warming the unbreakable smile on my face, was that adventuresome, pioneer blood that couldn't wait to get back to the wild again! With a freezer full of delicious elk meat, which was eventually shared with hundreds of people and helped raise thousands of dollars for charitable causes, and with the rack of the magnificent Miracle Bull proudly (the good kind of pride) displayed on my wall, the hunt of a lifetime had come full circle. And once again, the greatest "trophy" of all was making new friends, carving new trails in new lands, and sharing it all with the Lord God Almighty!

The Capitalization of Dreams

As I mentioned earlier, bowhunting elk had been one of my biggest dreams — but for the life of me, I can't pinpoint exactly when the seed was planted. There is no specific, initial memory in my thick skull that stands out as the birth-thought for my longing to hunt the majestic Rocky Mountain elk. It just seems to have always been there.

Perhaps the desire came from reading all those hunting magazines as a kid, or from seeing elk mounts on the walls of archery and barber shops (all those old-time barbers were out-doorsmen). Maybe it came from watching Saturday morning outdoor shows or nature/wildlife programs on TV, or from science class in school. I don't know. But the primordial sound of a bugling bull elk has echoed through the sonic chambers of my soul for as long as I can remember. Whenever I hear it, I go through some kind of instant, interior metamorphosis. I have an uncontrollable craving to bilocate to a cold mountaintop some-where way out in the Northwest and bugle back to the bull for all the world to hear, like the Angel Gabriel blowing his trumpet at the end of time! Mercy!

Of course, I'm not by any means the only person who has ever had such passionate feelings about elk hunting. I dare say that harvesting a mature bull elk (or any elk, for that matter) is the number one goal and dream of the vast majority of big game hunters, at least here in the Midwest, where I live.

The wapiti represents all that is wild, rugged, and free — and the land where he resides is likewise wild, rugged, and free. The elk embodies our American culture and history. They were of great importance to the Native Americans who hunted them for food and used their antlers, bones, and teeth for tools and decoration. Elk hides were used to make clothing, shelters, and blankets. These large, noble animals were an integral part of their way of life. The wapiti was also important to early Ameri-can settlers and explorers, such as Lewis and Clark, who con-sumed large quantities of elk meat during their travels and used the hides for clothing, shelter purposes, and gear as well.

This tradition continues as hunters today pursue the elk for food, for adventure, and for unforgettable memories. Yes, hunters obviously make use of the incredibly aesthetic antlers, hide, and ivory teeth, through taxidermy and other forms of craftsmanship, as a means of celebrating and immortalizing the animal and the hunt — but keep in mind, getting a huge set of antlers for the wall is not what it's all about. Hunting is a combination of adventure, stewardship, challenge, and sacred respect — not to mention darn hard work! As any *serious* hunter will attest to, the experience of the hunt, and all it encompasses, is the real "trophy."

Hunting, like any other pursuit in our country, is an activity where the dreams and desires of individuals are often capitalized on by resourceful folks who can aid in the actualization of those desires. The reality of this phenomenon — that a fantasy can, in fact, be fulfilled (for a price) — is what drives many people into developing not just a healthy desire, but a true lust for the fulfillment of their dream. The "price" of fulfilling a dream comes in many forms: money, hard work, sacrifice, or other such personal currency. There is always a price (good or bad) to be paid for success and satisfaction.

For many outdoorsmen, going on a big game adventure far away from home is often a once-in-a-lifetime opportunity. And once the realization and possibility of actually going on such an adventure becomes a reality, that rather latent, dormant desire, which has been brewing under the surface for years, comes to an explosive boil! The hunter says to himself:

> *Look at this ad I found in the back of my favorite hunting magazine! There is a place that will outfit and guide me on a hunt for only $$$$! It's a bit out of my budget for what I can spend on a vacation, but if I save up for five more years I could actually, possibly, do it! Oh boy! I can see myself now . . . riding on horseback through the big-sky country of Montana, scanning the lowlands for massive herd bulls, making a perfect shot with my new rifle, eating fresh elk steaks cooked over an open fire*

with Johnny West and company! Ahhh! I'm going to do it! I've
got to do it! Look out, elk country! Here I come!

Thus, after many years of scratching to make ends meet and
saving up every extra penny, the hunter coughs up some serious cash and hands it over to a multimillion-dollar, private-land,
"hunting ranch" operation, with the overdriven expectations of
having the hunt of a lifetime (obviously) but also of harvesting a
trophy animal. More desperate souls might even go to a "game
farm," where they can take a "trophy" that has been raised on a
small fenced-in pasture, is tame as the family dog, and comes
with a price tag that you don't even want to hear!

Yes, elk lust, along with any other kind of big game lust,
has driven many a good-souled hunter, who wants something
easier than a do-it-yourself hunt, into making a decision he and
his checkbook greatly regretted later — namely, an overpriced,
choreographed hunt that merely resembled the real thing.

Now don't get me wrong. A lot of these outrageously expensive "hunting ranch" operations do take place on huge expanses
of truly wild (though not public) land for truly wild animals,
not farm-raised transplants. Many of them do offer extremely
challenging hunts that would be no different from a "do-it-
yourself," state-land hunt. The only real difference is that the
private "ranch" hunts come with much more comfortable ame-
nities, cooked meals, and guides and assistants who do all the
backbreaking labor for you — and of course, that one's wallet
will be very skinny afterward.

Keep in mind also, though, that many a potential big game
hunter is a busy guy, with his hands full of family and work
responsibilities. He doesn't have the time or energy to do all
the planning and scouting required for an unguided, public-land
hunt, and he hasn't been blessed with a personal invitation, as I
most graciously was. His only option for fulfilling his dream is
to sign his name on a big fat check for a guided, fully outfitted

hunt. And really, if a hunter can actually afford it, that's perfectly fine. The point I'm simply making here is that such an endeavor will cost dearly — and that's the price of a capitalized dream, the price of things such as elk lust. And make no mistake: lust, of any kind, leads to bad things!

The Vice of Lust

As I mentioned earlier, this phenomenon of realizing that a fantasy can actually become a reality for a price applies to virtually anything. Whatever the desire one has — whether it's catching a trophy fish, going to Paris, losing 90 pounds, playing for the NFL ... you name it — if and when one realizes that there is, in fact, a rather immediate way for it to become reality, then that initial, dormant desire multiplies by a million! A slight spark of hope turns into a blazing wildfire inferno! It's then that the once-healthy desire becomes emblazoned with lust!

Lust is that which spurs one on to do things that are simply not good in order to fulfill an overdriven desire. It tempts one to selfishly attain pleasure by doing things like sacrificing one's integrity and worth, spending way too much money, lying, cheating, stealing, manipulating, and so on. Lust is a vice (like all the others) that leads to other vices. Lust can especially lead to various forms and expressions of gluttony and greed, as we saw back in Chapter 7.

Technically, *lust* can be defined as a disordered, inverted desire or craving for self-gratification and pleasure at the expense of one's self and others. Though lust is often referred to regarding sexual desires and pleasures, it can apply to any desire. Some have a genuine lust (not just a strong desire) for shopping, a lust for food, a lust for adventure, a lust for money, etc. When a natural, healthy desire crosses the line and becomes an unnatural, self-gratifying, out-of-control lust, it then leads to all sorts of destructive abuses of self and others.

For the rest of this chapter, I'll discuss the vice of lust as it applies to one's sexuality. So for starters, we see that we human beings, along with all the other creatures our Lord designed, were made with a natural attraction to members of the opposite sex. On the most basic level, without this built-in attraction, the human race (and life in general) would cease to exist. It's part of God's plan for a man to be physically attracted to a woman, and vice versa.

If there was no initial physical attraction (as well as intellectual and spiritual attraction) between a man and a woman, they would not pursue a relationship. And if a relationship was not pursued, their love would not grow and flourish, and thus it would not eventually reach the pinnacle of its fulfillment in the commitment of marriage and the expression of sexual intercourse, as is God's will. And if this sexual expression was not pleasurable, fulfilling, unifying, and life-giving, not too many couples would have a desire for it. And if that was the case, there would ultimately not be any offspring, which would result in mankind negating itself (which is already happening through abortion and various means of artificial contraception). God knew what he was doing in designing all this stuff, even though so many people have taken advantage of it and abused this great gift for selfish, sinful motives.

As every married person knows, the temptation toward sexual sin does not miraculously go away with the proclamation of one's wedding vows. That temptation does not go away for priests (like me) who have made a promise of celibacy, either. Everybody experiences sexual temptations to varying degrees. And as I've stated several times in my other books, out of all the temptations that are out there, out of all the sins that can really shatter lives, break relationships, and cause severe emotional, spiritual, and at times physical trauma, sexual sins would have to be at the top of the list. They ruin people's lives, their self-worth, their dignity, their trust, and their hope like nothing else can.

One of the major roots or causes of lustful sexual temptation and sin is *covetousness*. To *covet* is to wrongfully desire something with no regard for the rights and dignity of the other. To take it a step deeper, the primary source of our covetousness is our eyes. Our eyes hunt down the things we desire — and when those desires become overdriven, they turn into lust, which leads not to fulfillment, but to ruination and perpetual emptiness.

Living a life fueled by lust is like trying to catch a trophy rainbow trout out of the Lower Mississippi River. Sure, the fishing may be adventurous and fun, but that trout will never be caught. One will never experience the satisfaction of such a catch, because there simply is no trout there in the first place! When we try to fill a deep void in our life (like the need for true love) with fleeting, destructive things such as sins of lust, the void just gets deeper and deeper. As we saw earlier, the only thing that will fill the voids and the emptiness in our life is the love, the truth, and the life that is found in and from God.

Sins of Lust

When we look at sins of lust, we see that there are many. There is fornication — that is, sexual activity outside of a committed, loving relationship in the sacred covenant of marriage. In fornication, one uses the other person as a plaything for his or her own selfish pleasure, and then tosses the person aside when finished. It's a blatant act of dehumanization that tears apart the unity and dignity of the human person and steals away the genuine love, care, intimacy, and (again) commitment that should come from sexual intercourse.

In many cases, fornication results in the destruction of human life, through abortion or the "morning-after pill," when there is an unwanted pregnancy. In effect, the fornicator says to the other person: "I love you as much as the steak I had for dinner — and when I'm done consuming your flesh for my own pleasure, I'll throw your bones in the garbage." Yes, I know it's a bit extreme to put things like that. And while it may not be the actual intention of the fornicator, it is the reality, the truth, and the essence of such an act.

Another major sin driven by lust is the use of, or participation in, pornography. (Strip clubs and the like can be thrown into this category as well). Here again, the human person is turned into nothing more than a piece of meat for the pleasure of others who seek out that individual, like vultures circling a festering carcass. The pornography industry is one that thrives on and manufactures abuse, addiction, corruption, exploitation, enslavement, and absolute poison like no other. In pornography, a human being, who is made in the image and likeness of God, is reduced to something less than an animal for the purpose of selfish, immeasurably destructive pleasure.

Pornography demeans not only its subjects but its viewers as well. It transforms one into a moral degenerate and leads to even more destructive behavior and mental mind-sets. It trains and conditions one to substitute a healthy, real relationship with another human being for a false, nonexistent sense of intimacy between the subject and the viewer. It destroys what should be the healthy dynamics of human relationships and replaces them with a disordered fantasy life that only focuses on body parts.

In the various forms of "adult entertainment" (what a lie that is!), the great, life-giving gift of sexuality is violently unwrapped, torn asunder, and mocked in the most foul, ungrateful manner possible. It's interesting to note that the word "porno" comes from a Greek word meaning "that which should not be seen" — and this really sums it up. So many good men and woman of all ages get addicted to pornography, especially on the Internet, and find themselves unable to break free from its poisonous spell. It rots their souls and ruins their lives, their marriages, and their dignity. In a sense, the participation in or the use of pornography is a form of prostitution — which is, obviously, another serious sexual sin — in that one pays (either with money or personal dignity) for sexual pleasure. Here we see the true darkness of capitalizing on a desire.

The use of pornography in its various forms is like throwing gasoline on a fire. It can be difficult, under normal circumstances, to temper one's sexual desires. But when one is subjected to the most graphic sexual images possible, that desire becomes an out-of-control wildfire of lust, and it often destroys any remaining bit of self-control one may have had. When self-control is shattered; when the will is broken like a rotting twig underfoot; when one's passions and temptations are unleashed like a ravenous pit bull from hell — all this leads to the frantic hunger to quench the fire of lust by whatever means are quick and readily available. Thus, many good people do bad things when driven by the supercharged vice of lust.

Another of the most common sexual sins, besides fornication and pornography, is masturbation. We could spend an entire chapter just on this. But the bottom line is that, in masturbation, one becomes a sexual thief, along with turning his or her body into an amusement park. It's a disordered use of one's sexual organs, selfishly seeking and stealing away the pleasure that is meant for the true expression of unifying, life-giving, sacred love between a married couple in intercourse. The combination of masturbation and pornography is an addiction that plagues countless millions in our culture. It lowers one's self-esteem and one's sense of self-worth in one fell swoop.

I hear constantly from married men and women who struggle with this deadly duo; from young people who are enslaved to it; even from older folks who can't break free of the shackles of sexual impurity with self. I hear from wives who feel like dirt, unwanted and undesirable, because their husbands are more interested in the computer than in them. I also hear from husbands who resort to porn use because their wives have become unaffectionate and cold, or are interested in men other than them. The results of porn use and masturbation are that they take a serious toll on married and family life — after all, it's an act of mental adultery (adultery being another obvious sexual sin).

Those who are begrudgingly enslaved to these sins feel worthless, helpless, and powerless over their captivity to this powerful vice, which can only be broken by the grace of God, prayer, personal accountability, exercise of the will, and in some extreme cases, the help and support of a sex-addiction counselor or support group. And if you honestly need that level of help and support, then for God's sake don't be a fool. Get the help you need! True weakness is expressed in *not* asking for help. It takes strength to lay aside your deceiving pride and get the assistance you need.

Other sexual sins such as rape, sodomy, incest, and any form of sexual abuse or misuse are self-explanatory, not to mention punishable by law. But another big issue that comes up today quite often is that of homosexuality. I addressed this quite thoroughly in my book *Meat & Potatoes Catholicism*. But in case you missed that one, let me recap a few things on the subject.

The "gay lifestyle" is promoted and being "celebrated" with great enthusiasm in our culture today. There are TV shows, mainstream magazines, radio programs, and even entire media networks that cater to and revolve around homosexuals. Of course, many in our society see this as a great social advancement and a huge leap forward for diversity and acceptance for gays. Meanwhile, anyone who says or thinks otherwise is aggressively labeled as an ultraconservative, closed-minded, backwards, homophobic monster.

Here are some of the common arguments. "Homosexuality is natural; people are born with that inclination." "Individuals have a right to live as they choose and to love whom they want." "Politics and religion should not restrict two loving adults from entering into a marital union." "Science proves that homosexuality is not a disorder."

For starters, there are lots of scientific and psychological studies on the causes of homosexuality, and none of them are as yet conclusive. Homosexuality may be caused by some biological factors. Or it may be caused by social conditioning, such as growing up in a dysfunctional household with improper role models or negative experiences with persons of the opposite sex. In some cases, people are seduced or coerced into the gay lifestyle, and in other cases it is a freely chosen personal decision to live an "alternative lifestyle" by the people themselves.

Some ask, "Why would someone choose to be gay and take on all the trouble that comes with that lifestyle?" I don't know the answer to that question. But from my experience of hearing confessions, I can soundly verify that this is, in fact, the case with many homosexuals. There are studies out there to back up any argument one attempts to make regarding issues of homosexuality. That being the case, I'll limit my comments to common sense, objective truth, and the Word of God.

First of all, the Church does not teach that "God hates gays" or that people of the same sex can't have a loving, committed relationship. The issue is how that "love" is expressed. (I'm going to get a bit graphic here, so please be prepared.) The bottom line, which many people don't want to face and hear, is this: homosexual acts ("expressions of love"), such as anal and oral sex, are *not* healthy, holy, natural, or life-giving. They are, by their very definition, gravely, objectively disordered. Those body parts were not made to go together — and when they are forced, terrible things happen. It's as simple as a basic plumbing lesson.

These acts are not *naturally* unitive, and they do not foster life. As we've seen, the ultimate expression of committed love (sexual intercourse) between a man and a woman not only unites the couple physically, emotionally, and spiritually — and not only brings life and fulfillment to the couple — but is also biologically ordered to bring about new human life: a child. Think about that: an act of love having the power to bring new life into the world. Awesome! Now how can one possibly compare that with two homosexuals engaging in things like anal sex? Absurd! Such unnatural acts only bring about pain, disease, and death. The same applies to heterosexuals engaging in these acts.

The homosexual lifestyle (and yes, the promiscuous heterosexual lifestyle) is self-negating. In reality, it is a not a "lifestyle," but rather a *death*style. The millions dying from AIDS and other sexually transmitted diseases (STDs) give clear witness to this. When one has to use multiple forms of "protection" when engaging in sexual activity, and when there is the real threat of death, disease, or unwanted pregnancy (for heterosexuals), it should be clear that it's not a good idea to be engaging in such an act in the first place. It's sheer madness!

Contrary to public opinion, the Church is not a group of homophobic old folks trying to make life miserable for people who struggle with *same-sex attraction* (which is the essence of homosexuality). In fact, there are programs and organizations in place that minister to those struggling with same-sex attractions: Courage (*www.couragerc.net*) and Exodus International (*www.exodus-international.org*).

The Church's message is to not let our culture label one as "gay" and thus encourage all the negative attributes that go with it. When that happens, all hope is removed. Just as with same-sex attractions, there are those who are *born* with a disposition toward violence, extreme aggression, depression, and so on. A psychotic killer acts in accordance with his "natural" thought processes and desires. Is this a good thing that should be encouraged? No.

There are those who are *conditioned* by their environment and upbringing to use drugs and alcohol abusively. Should this abuse be celebrated with parades? No. There are those who *choose* to live a life of crime. Should it simply be ignored and thought of as an alternative way of living? No. It would be like telling someone who's trying to quit smoking: "You're a smoker. You'll never be able to give it up or live a healthy life, so go ahead and smoke yourself into oblivion." Or like saying to an alcoholic, "Well, you were born with an unstoppable craving for alcohol, and that's simply a part of who you are — so drink up!"

The point in all this is that it really doesn't matter if a disorder is either present at birth, conditioned, or chosen. It remains a disorder. It is not justified by cause. And again, homosexual sex, by its objective definition and nature, is gravely disordered.

So, what does God have to say on the issue? There are many passages in Scripture that deal with homosexuality, but one that really hits the nail on the head is found in the letter of St. Paul to the Romans, where we read this:

> Claiming to be wise, they became fools, and exchanged the glory of the immortal God for images resembling mortal man. . . . Therefore God gave them up in the lusts of their hearts to impurity, to the dishonoring of their bodies among themselves, because they exchanged the truth about God for a lie and worshiped and served the creature rather than the Creator, who is blessed for ever! Amen.
>
> For this reason God gave them up to dishonorable passions. Their women exchanged natural relations for unnatural, and the men likewise gave up natural relations with women and were consumed with passion for one another, men committing shameless acts with men and receiving in their own persons the due penalty for their error. (Rom 1:22-23, 24-27)

That about says it all — and notice that one of the key factors is "the *lusts* of their hearts."

The Loss of the Sense of Sin

To get back on track a bit here, we've now seen the many possible evil avenues that lust can lead one to. But so many people don't even realize that they're being "eaten alive," or that their soul is decaying like the rotting flesh of a leper as a result of their rampant sexual sin. They haven't comprehended how truly sick with vice they have become. This phenomenon is the direct result of another: the loss of the sense of sin, which brings about the loss of a sense of God.

In our culture today, nothing seems to be a sin anymore. We're told that adultery, fornication, homosexual acts, pornography, and such things are not sins; they are one's "lifestyle choices." Abortion is not the murderous destruction of an unborn human being; it's a "choice." (A choice that kills!) Our culture preaches that cheating, lying, deceit, and manipulation are not offenses against God and our neighbor, but that they are simply "business strategies." Drug abuse? No, no, no ... don't you mean "performance enhancement?" The rationalization and denial go on and on, and as a result we keep ourselves blinded from seeing the truth and coming to know that the only cure for our sickness is "the way, the truth, and the life" that is found in God, who offers us forgiveness, healing, and freedom from our sins.

The Virtue of Chastity

The cure for the vice of lust that God offers us is the virtue of chastity. Now, probably for most people, when they hear the word "chastity" they think of it as simply meaning not ever having sex — and who in their right mind wants that? But this is not necessarily what the true meaning of chastity is. *Chastity* is the proper use of our sexuality in accordance with our particular state in life. It leads us to guard our hearts and minds from evil influences and allows us to love freely and purely, without the enslavement of addiction and vice.

For a married couple, the "proper use" of their sexuality is, as we've already discussed, to express, to unify, and to bring life and the fulfillment of love to their relationship. It's also a means of being open to, and working with, God in bringing new life into the world, to "be fruitful and multiply," as we hear in Genesis (1:28). When sexual intercourse between a married couple becomes nothing more than a self-seeking act to gratify one's self at the other's expense, it enters into the realm of sin. There are many married people out there who simply "use" their spouse for their own sexual pleasure and really couldn't care less about any kind of expression of genuine love or real intimacy — and this is truly sinful.

For those who are not married, being chaste means to be a good steward of the powers of life and love that are within, and to not exploit those gifts or use them out of the proper context. For the single person (or those who have taken a vow of celibacy), chastity is a way of expressing life and love in non-sexual ways. Intercourse (or any kind of sexual activity) is not by any means the only way to express healthy intimacy and love for another. To be chaste also means to live a life of "self-mastery," to exercise discipline and self-control, and to temper one's passions and not let the vice of lust, and the sins that come from it, make one a helpless captive.

As we all know, however, avoiding sexual temptation is more difficult than ever in our sex-saturated society. Sexual sin originates in our mind — thus, we must use our brainpower as the first line of defense to make a real effort to avoid the *near occasions of sin* (that is, the things that we know good and well will lure us into the temptations we most likely will not be able to resist).

We must be vigilant in practicing things such as "custody of the eyes." One of the greatest defenses we have against covetousness and temptations of all kinds is our eyelids! Another great defense is the "Off" button on the remote control or the "Power" button on the computer. You have the "power" (with the grace of God) to exercise mastery over temptation — so use it well! Just as when a big ol' bull elk gets a whiff of human odor and gets the heck out of the area immediately, we, too, have to flee the dangers of sexual sin and temptation with that same degree of purpose and instinct.

Another point to keep in mind is that there is a big difference between *admiration of beauty* and *lust* — though it can, at times, be a dangerously fine line! True admiration of beauty is not evil; the Lord made some very beautiful people, and the world would be dull without them. But again, that line between admiration and lust is easy to cross. An old priest once gave me some great advice in this matter. He said:

> When you see a lovely lady, don't pretend she's not there. Thank and praise God for this beautiful person, but leave it at that. In doing so, you diffuse the work of the devil by turning an occasion of possible lust into a moment of glorifying God for his wonderful creation.

It's good advice that has worked for me!

As a final thought: Be vigilant! We must be prepared to do battle with temptation. We must exercise our God-given human dignity every day and be on guard against that which would steal it away and make us a slave to the flesh. Of course, there are those times that we may have fought a good fight, but still got our butts kicked by sin. Don't fret or despair! Get back up, go to the Lord to be washed clean and strengthened, and get back in the ring! Replace lust with love, temper it with chastity (just as a mighty sword is tempered for strength), and claim victory in the battle against vice!

Chapter 9

LAZY BUM!

FROM TIME TO TIME, one will hear fantastic (though initially dubious) stories, like that of a young kid who, on his first fishing trip, caught a new-state-record rainbow trout with his Snoopy rod and reel, using a stale, day-old cheese fry as bait — or the tale of a monster buck being taken by someone's wife who's never spent more than two hours in the woods before. When the validity of such tales is actually confirmed, we commonly call these occurrences "luck," or even one better: "dumb luck." I've heard it said that there is no such thing as luck — at least not as we usually tend to think of it — but rather "luck is when skill and opportunity meet." Personally, I've always liked that particular definition.

Yet one is still left asking this question: "What, then, of those who are not very skilled and were simply in the right place at the right time, and by no credit of their own, quite honestly, just happened to pull the trigger at the proper moment, or miraculously didn't break the line while clumsily manhandling a substantially humongous fish on cheap, inadequate gear?" Some call such circumstances a "fluke," "fortune," or an "accident," while others say it was a "blessing." In the big picture, it doesn't really matter how one wants to label such happenings: the fact remains, they do indeed happen.

Probably everyone reading this book has had such an occurrence at least one time in his or her life in some area. Maybe you won a rich, delectable, coconut cream pie at a county fair simply by having your name or ticket pulled out of a big grubby hat by a large man dressed in a purple gorilla suit. (Perhaps that same sugary, delicious pie humiliatingly ended up in your face while, still on your raffle-victory high, you weren't paying attention on the drive home, ran over a raccoon, swerved the car in a knee-jerk reaction, and smacked into a telephone pole! What are the chances of that?) Maybe on another occasion, you won 50 bucks with a lottery scratch-off ticket, or a new car by being the 100th person to walk through the door of a new auto dealership in town. While not displaying or utilizing an ounce of skill in any way, shape, or form — and perhaps not even being aware of any such opportunity — something very good happened.

While there is no doubt that luck or chance can fall upon anyone from time to time, there is also no doubt that those who are consistently the recipients of such good fortune do not just rely on mere accidental happenings. This holds true especially in the world of hunting and fishing. The individuals who regularly harvest exceptional animals or catch fish of noteworthy character do so because they know good and well what they are doing, and because they have done their homework and know how to apply certain principles to bring about certain results. They consciously, willfully, manufacture "luck" by developing their skills to the maximum potential, and by constantly taking advantage of the windows of opportunity that come along, no matter how big or small, fast or slow, they may be. They *make* skill and opportunity meet.

The Consistently Successful Outdoorsman

Let's take a moment now and have a good look at the characteristics that a consistently successful hunter/fisherman must possess.

First of all, one must obviously have an interest in the outdoors. In fact, it takes more than just interest — it takes true passion, and perhaps even obsession! One must have a desire to enter into the natural world on a much higher level than that of a mere spectator. One must understand the paradox of taking life, which obviously takes place in hunting and fishing; it is sad to see a beautiful animal die. It is not fun to watch the spark of life dwindle away from a creature's eye, knowing that you are responsible for it. But there is satisfaction, and yes, even a sense of joy, in having become an active participant in the cycle of life and having harvested an animal or fish with a humane kill, true respect, sacred reverence, and deep gratitude.

A governing rule of life on earth is that something must die for something else to live. Hunters and fishermen know firsthand the price their food paid; thus, they foster a sense of the sacred in what they do and what they eat. As that spark of life fades from our quarry's eyes, it enlightens and sustains the spark in ours. As Jesus reminds us, "Unless a grain of wheat falls into the earth and dies, it remains alone; but if it dies, it bears much fruit" (Jn 12:24). Death gives way to life in more ways than one. If a hunter's or fisherman's killing only gives way to death, then it's time to hang it up. A serious outdoorsman must live by these principles.

Along with developing a deep interconnectedness to the natural world, and fostering the sacred respect it deserves, one must acquire outdoor knowledge, and lots of it. The more one knows, the better one's "chances" are for success. One of the alluring characteristics (at least for me) about the outdoors is that the sky is the limit, as far as the challenges and opportunities for growth are concerned. There is always more to learn about wildlife behavior, about their habitat, food sources, life cycles, etc. Learning to read the water, studying "structure" (habitat), investigating a fish's diet, and knowing the biology of that fish's preferred prey are things one could easily spend a lifetime doing.

Becoming intimately familiar with how temperature, weather conditions, and moon phases affect fish and wildlife is a science in itself. All of these factors are what *create* opportunities for success, and the accomplished outdoorsman hunts for these things, as much as for his quarry. Then, of course, don't forget that one must have a memorized knowledge of the laws, rules, and regulations that apply to hunting and fishing and to the lands on which these activities are pursued — not to mention, one must know about outdoors survival, first aid, and other information of that sort, in the event that things go terribly wrong.

Besides the endless opportunities for intellectual growth that the outdoors provides, it also *demands* proficiency within the ways of marksmanship. One simply must be able to hit the target. Sure, we all miss from time to time, or make a bad shot. Nobody is perfect. But still, one must have polished his/her skills to as near perfection as possible. We owe it to the game we pursue to make a quick, clean, humane, lethal kill.

Hunters must never cease practicing with their preferred weapon. Going out to the range the weekend before the hunting season opens and shooting a few times does not cut it! We must practice in all different shooting positions, while wearing different kinds of clothes and gear, at different yardages, in different weather conditions, and still be equally deadly in all. One would never expect an ex-professional boxer to come out of retirement and simply knock out the current heavyweight champion without any training. The same principle applies to hunters: year-round expertise with our gear and the ongoing honing of our skills is a must.

This proficiency also applies to fishing. One must be able to delicately, accurately present a fly or lure with pinpoint accuracy. One must be able to flip or cast bait to an exact spot without error in certain situations. Failure to do so can mean the difference between a hookup with the fish of a lifetime or another story of the "one that got away."

In order to be consistently successful in the woods and on the water, there is also the physical factor. Today, thankfully, there are many opportunities for disabled hunters and for those who are not in the best of shape (for one reason or another). But if one truly desires to pursue all the challenges the outdoors has to offer, and to lovingly take on the fury and incessant beating that Mother Nature can dish out, then he or she has to be in the best possible physical condition. When the ATV trails come to an abrupt end and one's feet are the only mode of transportation, those feet simply can't be weighted down by an extra 50 pounds of blubber and beer gut, especially if one is planning to do things like stalk trout all day over thousands of yards of water, or drag a significantly heavy animal out of the deep dark woods where man is not welcome.

On top of all this, one also must possess the proper virtues that success demands. The accomplished hunter or fisherman must be patient … very patient! Waiting for hours on end, hiking for miles upon miles, or working over a particular stretch of water for what seems like eternity is often the price that must be paid. Thus, one must have the disciplined physical, mental, and spiritual currency to pay the price. One must also be humble enough to recognize his or her own faults and failings, and to learn from them, instead of getting flustered or aggravated, and then quitting like the proverbial big crybaby.

The Need for Diligence

For the consistently successful outdoorsman, the one virtue that must stand out above the rest and become one's modus operandi is *diligence*. This is what leads to ultimate success again and again. Diligence is also, perhaps, one of the hardest virtues to instill, and to nurture into growth and maturity. It's just plain difficult to keep at something with dogged determination and perpetual perseverance when every attempt appears to fail and victory seems absolutely impossible. When the odds are far from being stacked in one's favor, it may seem genuinely insane to keep at it no matter what. However, it's the implementation of diligence that will, sooner or later, bring about success; one simply cannot be slothful in any way. Laziness must become the enemy!

I can quite vividly recall one particular deer (firearms) season when diligence paid off big time. Even though bowhunting is my true love, I still go out for the firearms season, just for the sake of getting out there — and more so, for the camaraderie with hunting buddies. Well, this one particular season opened with a perfect morning: cold, still, and overcast. I was hunting on a farm (known in secret code as the "MNWA") that had at least a few big, mature bucks. And so, when a nice, fat, healthy-looking doe came by, to within absurdly easy shooting range, I let her walk on, to see if one of the big dudes was hot on her trail. Wouldn't you just know it: that was not the case. As I watched that perfect specimen of an exceptionally large whitetail doe go casually tiptoeing by, I began to wonder if I just broke the golden rule of hunting: *Never pass up on the first day what you'd gladly take on the last!*

After that opening day, things got crazy! The conditions became windy as could be, terribly warm, and all sorts of insane Midwestern weather patterns came through, causing deer movement to shut down almost completely. I didn't see hide nor hair of a whitetail for the rest of the weekend, nor did almost anyone else I knew. Over the next few outings, it either rained like the dickens, continued to be obnoxiously windy, or got so blasted cold that the deer bedded down tight (to conserve body heat) and didn't move until midday. To top it off, I missed a shot on a big deer as a result of misjudging the yardage. It was one thing after the next!

During the middle of the season, I did get in a successful bowhunt — unfortunately, a pack of hungry coyotes ate the better part of my deer and left me with a nasty, stinking mess of venison leftovers. Darn coyotes! I just couldn't seem to win.

Finally, on the last day of the extended gun season, during the last hour of the hunt, after days and days of fruitless hunting, after hours and hours of seeing absolutely nothing, I harvested a nice big, considerably portly, Missouri doe during a hunt that took place right after a massively destructive ice storm. Like a complete idiot, I stayed right out in it. I just couldn't help myself. It was a painfully bitter cold day that about killed me! It was the kind of hunt that makes one into an old man well before his time. And wouldn't you know it: the deer that I harvested that day looked just like the one I passed up on opening morning!

A bitterly cold hunt and the "Doe of Diligence"

It was diligence, and diligence alone, that kept me motivated to continue the hunt no matter what — and it was that same diligence that was responsible for filling the freezer that season.

The Lazy Bum
Let me shift gears for a moment now and do a bit of self-revealing here. This "consistently successful outdoorsman" I've been speaking of is certainly not me — though, Lord knows, I'm diligently trying! For example, most of the time when my overly complicated alarm clock sounds off in the wee hours of the morning, I respond to that much dreaded sound not with instant tenacity, but rather with a sonance of my own, which goes something like this: "Uuugggrgaahhhh."

As I pry my usual dry-mouthed, haggard, pillow-creased face from a prone position, and with raspy knuckles wipe the weariness from my eyes, I start my day by fumbling around, trying to find the snooze button. After a series of trial-and-error attempts, pressing one of the many similar buttons on the clock, I finally find it and try to imagine it was all a dream, and that I, in fact, didn't hear that wake-up call. But it's no use. I know, in fact, that it's time to get up. With another groan of discontentment, I eventually sit up, wait for the blood to start flowing some, and then stand up and begin my usual morning ritual of readiness.

As much as I cherish and appreciate the morning, especially in the great outdoors, I have to admit that I'm simply not a "morning person." As a priest, I almost always have to begin my days fairly early, and there are consistently a number of things I must attend to well before the morning commute begins. The truth is, though, I simply don't function well in the morning. I don't think straight. I often feel fatigued and sluggish. God only knows how I have tried to convert myself into a morning person over the years, but it has been to no avail. I've attempted to implement all sorts of regimens to get myself more attuned to life in the a.m., but for the most part, those attempts have been dismal failures. On most days, the grace of God and a good, strong cup of coffee are my primary motivators as the sun begins its ascent.

For various reasons, moderate sleep deprivation seems to be a way of life for me. And so, the older I get, the more I appreciate, and long for, a good night's rest. Part of the reason for my difficulty sleeping is that I can't seem to shut off my mind at night. As soon as my head hits the pillow, no matter how tired I may be, my brain kicks into hyperspeed, and I start processing information and thinking about all sorts of things. I'll kick around thoughts of how to solve or address particular ministerial issues. I'll critique my work performance, or meditate on different creative ideas. I'll think about the problems parishioners are facing or about the assortment of projects that need to be worked on.

On and on, the thoughts and ideas just keep coming in an endless stream. Then I start to get aggravated. I say to myself: *All right! That's enough! I'll deal with it later. Now get to sleep, dang it!*

It's usually then, through my red squinty eyes, that I take a quick glance at those haunting, illuminated numbers on the alarm clock. *Midnight? Go to sleep!*

Then the dreaded insomnia race begins: me versus the clock. *All right, I'm going to be asleep in 15 minutes*, I try to convince myself. I hurriedly go through a series of relaxation exercises — counting sheep, doing deep breathing, and all the rest — but I soon find myself taking a look at the clock again, only to find another hour has slipped by, and I'm still wide awake and now angrily fuming over my defeat. Somehow, I do finally slip off to slumberland, and when the alarm sounds in the morning . . . well . . . we've already covered that — and it's not pretty!

Even on the night before a day off, I'll have a hard time sleeping, but that's because I'm so terribly excited about the next day. I lie there in bed, smiling like a giddy kid and thinking to myself:

> *Oh boy, oh boy, oh boy! I'm going fishing tomorrow! I can't wait! Weee-heee! I can see the river already! I wonder if I'll catch that huge brown trout that's been lurking around? Maybe I should head out there right now! They are primarily nocturnal feeders, after all! Will the morning ever come?*

Of course, the morning does finally come, and though I'm bursting with excitement and seem to get moving quite a bit faster, I still feel lousy for the most part. However, as my blood gets pumping, I simply transform myself into an unstoppable fishing/hunting machine, and I consciously will away the fatigue and enjoy the day to the fullest.

Insomnia is a vicious cycle, but thankfully it doesn't plague me nearly as much as it did in years past. I've made tremendous improvements in my quest, and need, for a good night's sleep. But let me be totally honest with you: I sometimes use my sleeping troubles as an excuse and a way to rationalize. Truth be told, at times I'm simply a lazy bum! Many mornings I hit that snooze button not out of genuine need, but because I just don't *feel* like getting up. I procrastinate to the last possible second, instead of being diligent and vigilantly getting on with my morning duties.

Sometimes (though not all that often, really) I use the excuse of not getting enough sleep to justify my not attending to things that I should: *Poor me. I'm soooo tired. I deserve a break.* And so, as I drink a big, black, bitter, murky, steaming cup of self-pity, I let myself off the hook for my pathetic acts of sloth. Again, such laziness is not the norm for me, and I've *never* intentionally missed something that I absolutely was obliged to do. But in other areas where there is some wiggle room, I'll admit that sloth (not the three-toed, South American mammal, mind you) has gotten the best of me from time to time.

Laziness: the fastest way to failure!

Let me tell you, too, that I've paid the price many a time for my laziness, especially in my outdoor pursuits. On more than one occasion, I got up several hours later than I'd originally planned, and by the time I made it to the woods or the waters, all activity was done for the day. I've missed more than a few fishing or hunting "prime times" because I just didn't feel like getting up yet — and like that ol' blind, loathsome mole digging in the dirt, I rolled around in my covers desperately trying to block out the morning light instead of getting up and at 'em. Make no mistake, though: there is rarely a time that I haven't terribly regretted my bouts of laziness.

I'll also have to admit (as my hunting buddies know) that there is the occasional missing of a morning hunt due to *intentional* sleep deprivation — that is, when one is up until 2 a.m., telling jokes, reminiscing, and hootin' and hollerin' around a campfire. Every now and then, my diligence goes right up in smoke like a chunk of dry driftwood!

After I finally get out of bed on those embarrassing days and walk out into the refreshing late-morning air, I say to myself: *Man, what was I thinking? What an awesome day! And I've already wasted half of it! Joey ol' boy, you did it again! You lazy bum, you!*

To make matters worse, on those rare occasions when I engage in such antics, someone will come back to camp for an early lunch and say something like: "Wow! You really missed out! I've never seen so much deer activity in all my life! Huge bucks were chasing does all over the place! And the biggest one was headed right in the direction of your area ... which you weren't in!" It's then that I hang my head low in disgust, that I see the virtue of diligence squashed and crushed like an empty beer can, and I hear those humiliating words ring out for all the universe to hear: "And the winner by knockout, and still champion of the world — sloth!"

Laziness and Sloth

Like some of the other seven deadly sins, sloth is not so much a vice or a sin in its initial stage. It is more of a circumstance that gives way to sin. *Sloth* is essentially the avoidance of work (physical, mental, or spiritual). Sloth is a failure to use one's abilities and to *not* actualize the potential of one's gifts and talents. Attached to this vice is a general lack of concern about one's responsibilities or other important matters. On the spiritual level, it is a failure to seek and then do the will of God — which ultimately affects our salvation. It is seeking a life of ease and comfort, instead of being willing to put forth a maximum effort in striving to live a virtuous life and (with the grace of God) overcoming the captivity of sin.

An attitude of laziness runs rampant in our culture today on all levels and in all areas of life. As I often mention, America is a country of *extremes*. Just look at how much that word is used. We have *extreme* sports, *extreme* soft drinks, *extreme* music, *extreme* makeovers, *extreme* cars, *extreme* everything. There are those who are extremely conservative and those who are extremely liberal, extremely moral or extremely sinful, extremely wealthy or extremely poor. It is also easy to see that in America there are those who are extremely hardworking and those who are extremely lazy.

Many Americans work their fingers to the bone and turn their minds into mush with exhaustion. Some have to do so to make ends meet and provide for their families, and others do so out of their lust for extreme wealth and an extremely lavish lifestyle at all costs.

On the other hand, there are those who are extremely lazy, who are purposely underemployed, or who don't work at all and just expect a handout. Many Americans want to get paid for doing virtually nothing, while expecting the best, but they lack the desire to work hard to support themselves or their families. Unfortunately, there are more than just a few individuals in our land who couldn't care less about accomplishing or pursuing anything constructive or worthwhile and just go through life comfortably cooking in the stew of their own sloth. To be sure, that stew might be nice and warm, but it's also lacking any nourishment and leaves one empty, in need, and in a state of perpetual ruination.

Such laziness gives way to seeking shortcuts in life, and also to cheating, stealing, lying, and various criminal activities — all of which only lead down the path to trouble, and possibly to time behind bars. There is no doubt that extremely poor social and economic conditions experienced during childhood greatly influence a person's level of diligence. When the odds of ever getting ahead — which includes receiving a good education, learning marketable skills, and attaining a decent job — seem impossible at best, it's also likely there will be a serious lack of motivation to get out of that situation and rise above it.

There is also the reality of being spoiled lazy. Again, there are more than a few Americans who have grown up in a thriving social and economic environment, in an atmosphere of great abundance, who, as a result, have been given the best educational and job opportunities the world has to offer. But some of them squander those opportunities and don't live up to their potential, failing not only to better themselves but also to improve the lives of others.

This apparent injustice, of course, enrages those on the other side of the spectrum. And that rage is often expressed in ways that are not so good, such as looking for those easy ways out and getting into trouble, or by turning the anger inward, resulting in a cycle of depression, abuse, addiction, and a general sustained sadness, which robs individuals of any encouragement.

The Remedy of Diligence

In any case, diligence is the key. The virtue of *diligence* is the readiness and willingness to do whatever it takes and whatever is needed to achieve a goal. It is the fire of persistence that cannot be extinguished by anyone or anything, no matter what! Just as the master outdoorsman never ever gives up the pursuit, and all that is involved with it, so this same principle applies to everything else in life: getting out of poverty and debt, earning a scholarship to a good school, becoming more suitably employed, finding a spouse, overcoming an addiction, etc. Success will only come with diligence — and like all other virtues, diligence comes directly from the grace of God.

There is one big, key factor in developing the virtue of diligence that must be kept in mind, though, and that is the power of faith. Without faith in what we are trying to achieve or accomplish, there is simply no point in pursing it and implementing diligence in the first place. If we simply do not believe that we can ever get out of a drug-infested, crime-ridden living environment, then we never will. If we don't have faith that we can actually get into a decent college and excel in our studies, then we won't.

If we don't know in our heart, without a shadow of a doubt, the possibility of success in what we seek, then it will never be found. The desire will never be realized; the potential will never be actualized. We will, instead, be left sitting at home, making excuses, putting the blame on someone else, rationalizing and victimizing ourselves (in more ways than one), all the while devouring the malnourishing stew of sloth and attempting to convince ourselves to be happy and content with being "comfortably numb."

Another point concerning faith: we often hear about the importance of "having faith in yourself." Well, that's good and fine to a point, but don't forget that it's often our *self* that has gotten us into a mess in the first place. Our self can be our greatest enemy and craftiest deceiver. One's faith must be rooted in something outside of, and be infinitely more powerful than, one's self. You guessed it: our faith should be rooted in the "higher power" of God Almighty.

The transforming power of the virtue of diligence is something that also applies to the spiritual life, naturally. As I often remind folks, the *will of God*, in its most basic form, on the most primary level, is the same for all: it is to love God with all one's mind, heart, and strength; to love one's neighbor as one's self; and to avoid sin, which destroys that love. Obviously, there is a lot that comes along in living out that rudimentary will. But in a nutshell, that's it. It can be quite easy for sloth to take hold of our mind and heart, and to weaken our strength, making us unable to live our life out of love for God and neighbor, all the while putting a massive damper on our motivation to strive for holiness and to live a sanctified life — that is, to put our faith into practice.

Sometimes we say things like this to ourselves:

> *I just don't feel like turning the other cheek today and being forgiving and merciful [as God is toward us]. I just don't care about my neighbor's problems or struggles; I've got plenty of my own. I'm simply not in the mood to pray and spend time with God. I honestly want to overindulge on _____ . It's not so bad once in a while. I'm just not going to give a few bucks to that charity or volunteer some time; I don't care who it benefits — nobody ever helps me out. If you need a helping hand, don't look to me — look at the end of your wrists!*

As people of faith, we, too, can easily fall into the trap of making excuses, rationalizing, and victimizing ourselves — and as a result, we fail to live out the will of God.

As important as it is to implement diligence in our lives, we also must help others to implement it in theirs and thereby build up the "Body of Christ." The readiness and willingness to do whatever it takes, and whatever is needed, to achieve a goal — and the mind-set of never ever giving up — don't just happen overnight. That fire does, in actuality, at times dwindle, if not burn out completely, for one reason or another. That is when we must encourage one another, out of love for God and neighbor, to carry on, to take the next step in the right direction, to get back in the ring, to go one more round, to get off one's lazy butt, and to get out of bed and take on the day. *Carpe diem!* — Seize the day!

As our Lord continues to pick us up off the floor and lift us up out of the mess we've made, so too, we are called to do the same for others: to be willing to lovingly exercise fraternal charity, to at least attempt to motivate our fellow man and throw out that rancid sloth stew. God knows that our words can only do so much. Sometimes our actions can only do so much. No matter how much we may try to get somebody headed in the right direction and fuel the fire of diligence in his or her life, there are times when the fire just won't light. And after we've done all we can do and said all we can say, we simply have to pray without ceasing and turn things over to the work and inspiration of the Holy Spirit and let his fire fall! His fire is one that, when received with a gracious heart and a mind of faith, can set the whole world on fire and burn away the slavery of sloth. So pray for that fire, let it burn hot in your heart, and be sure of one thing: when that fire is lit, the last thing you'll feel like doing is being a no-good, sittin' around, doin' nothing, lazy bum!

Chapter 10

SPIRITUAL SURVIVAL

ONE PARTICULAR EVENING, in the not-so-distant past, I found myself at a 50th wedding anniversary celebration. It was a wonderful event and an occasion of great joy to hear the testimonies and treasured memories of family and longtime friends of the well-endured bride and groom. The longevity of the happy couple's life together was an astounding witness to the true power and enduring fruitfulness of committed love.

After dinner, I found myself wandering aimlessly around the room, attempting to mingle with the assembled guests, which, admittedly, I always feel awkward doing. But nonetheless, I made the rounds and exchanged pleasantries and good cheer with the folks in attendance.

As I drifted toward the back of the room, I noticed an old man and his wife sitting with a few other couples. She was casually chitchatting away like all the rest, attempting to be heard over the rather loud ambience. But her husband seemed a bit different than the other fellows present that evening. He looked as if he secretly felt out of place, as I sort of did.

Amidst the clinking of delicate wineglasses and the mellow, piped-in, reminiscing music and the Salisbury steak, he had a downtrodden demeanor, with his thoughts seeming to be elsewhere. The patina of his aged, frosty gray hair slightly covered an obviously weather-beaten face that had been carved by the careful, though unrelenting hand of Mother Nature. His piercing, steel blue eyes stared through the veil of cultural complacency and were noticeably focused on something else, at another time, another place, far away from perfectly pressed white linen tablecloths, fine crystal, and polished silverware. He was noticeably miles apart from towering icing-covered cakes and martinis served in fancy glasses — shaken, not stirred, mind you!

As I casually conversed with the guests at his table, somehow the subject of hunting came up. (Imagine that!) Instantly, the old man's "talonous" hands released the shiny fork — with which he had been prodding the sauce-covered, highly processed meat — and he quickly looked up from his rather malaised stare, as if some kind of loathsome magic spell had been broken. As we locked eyes, we could read each other's mind. Before we ever spoke a word to each other, we seemed to be engaging in some sort of nonverbal communication, as if we were fellow aliens from another planet.

I knew exactly what he was thinking. I could see and understand his thoughts, which were as clear as the tell-tale waters of my favorite trout stream. A fire still burned behind those elderly eyes. I could see the reflection of the jagged mountain peaks he had hiked to and through. I could envision the winding rivers in the valleys below; the tall, green conifers that kissed the smoky sky; and the flickering of a warm campfire at the end of a very cold day. I could see the focus that his eyes once held as they looked for blood trails, as they strained to make out the twitching of a tail or the matte finish of an antler point protruding out of the thick, tangled cover. I perceived the joy that once lit up his soul, as he celebrated a successful hunt with his friends. I could also sense the tears of sadness he had shed over an animal never recovered, while wolves howled with unbridled delight throughout the bloody, starlit autumn night.

His hands bore the scars of many numb-fingered hide skinnings. His aching, arthritic knees reminded him of days past, spent pounding the treacherous turf in search of big game. The slight wheezing of his lungs bespoke the labor they once endured while climbing into the high, oxygen-starved environs that rejected mankind, but welcomed the creatures he pursued.

In his ears was a slight ringing from the percussion of one too many unprotected rifle rounds. But in his heart pumped a thick, rich, red blood that had humbly, gratefully, carried him to places most men have never dreamed of going, and doing things most men never have had the gumption to do. The tenderness in his otherwise overpowering eyes reflected a deep, sincere love for God, family, and compatriots. But still, there was a testimonial longing for the cold, thin air of the Western mountains; the majestic sound of bugling bulls; the gentle, hypnotic peace of an early fall rain shower; the euphoric splendor of a trickling stream; and the cascading descent of crisp, vibrantly colored, falling leaves.

As I spoke briefly with the rugged old gent, my intuitions and observations were confirmed. His life was one spent at the beck and call of the wild. He had indeed seen it all and done it all, spending death-defying weeks on Alaskan fishing boats; journeying through the Northwestern terrain in search of moose, antelope, mule deer, and elk; stalking the Midwest for elusive whitetails and eastern gobblers; and fishing the waters everywhere that flow throughout this great land. He had survived countless life-threatening dangers as a part of his many adventures. He nonchalantly, though quite seriously, mentioned that he was lucky to be alive. He didn't go into the details, but I knew it was no joke. Having endured years of so many quests, he no doubt had come face-to-face with death on more than one occasion.

Essentials for Outdoor Survival

For the typical, casual outdoors outing at one's local park or place of retreat, one must always be prepared for emergencies of one kind or another. No matter what the activity, or how seemingly harmless a day's plans, things can (and often do) go terribly wrong. Danger is always present in a multitude of forms — everything from automobile accidents to tick bites — and the consequences can vary from mild to deadly. However, when one takes the next step and decides to venture far, far beyond the pavement, miles upon miles away from hospitals, convenience stores, cell-phone signals, and gas stations, one's level of readiness and preparedness must decidedly exceed the norm. Your life (and perhaps the lives of others) is in your hands, and your hands alone. The term "fatal error" takes on a literal meaning. Take a look at the obituary section of an Alaskan newspaper and you'll see the reality of this, with, frequently, entry after entry of the unfortunate demise of ill-prepared adventurers, pseudo-outdoorsmen and would-be eco-warriors.

As the Boy Scouts say: "Be prepared!"

When we are in a place and a situation where the only helping hands are connected to our own forearms, we must know how to use them to survive. There are thousands of books, videos, and workshops that teach survival skills. But whether the outdoor activity of choice is backpacking, big game hunting, or wildlife photography, when we are genuinely immersed in the wild world, we must know how to stay alive, and thrive, when

optimum conditions go south in a hurry. When a life-threatening situation occurs, we must have the knowledge, the essential
equipment, and the skills to use that equipment in order to see
the light of another day.

I'm by no means a "survival expert." But I do know the
basics, and I'm constantly educating myself further. After reading many survival manuals and consulting the work of quite a
few true experts, there is what seems to be a list of 10 "must-
have" survival items. Now, some of these items are obviously
more important than others, and some will be more useful than
others, depending on the given situation. But they all are, nonetheless, *essential* for outdoor survival.

Before we take a look at these necessary items, it would be
good to first reflect upon the "Rule of Threes." *The rule states
that one can survive for* THREE MINUTES *without air,* THREE HOURS
without shelter (in threatening temperature extremes), THREE DAYS
without water, and THREE WEEKS *without food.* Keeping this rule
in mind is an imperative way to prioritize your survival plan. So
as long as you can breathe and have enough air, your top con-
cerns, in this order, are: shelter, water, food. Some professional
survivalists would, however, add fire to this list as well, since one
needs fire in many cases to stay warm, purify water, cook food,
etc. These folks recommend a prioritized plan of shelter, water,
fire, and then food, in that order. Now, we will just be scratching
the surface here, but let's move on and have a quick gander at the
essentials of survival gear. (By the way, these are in no particular
order here.)

First, you absolutely must have drinkable water to survive.
Without proper hydration, you will die — period! More than
two-thirds of your body is composed of water, and vital organs
(such as the brain) comprise as much as 85 percent water. Therefore, if you dry up, your time on earth is done. It's important to
keep in mind, too, that food is of no use if you do not have water
for the proper digestion and metabolizing of it. That being said,

you must make it a top priority to always have a sufficient supply of water and a means to purify more of it. This can be done in several ways: by boiling it, by using water-purifying tablets, or by having a compact filtration system.

Second, a compass is essential to find your way. Without it, you may wander around pointlessly in the wrong direction for hours or even days. Of course, you must also know how to use a compass, and it must be a trustworthy, quality product that will give an accurate reading. If your compass came out of a cereal box or is lodged in the butt-end of your "Rambo" knife, you might consider getting a more reliable model. There are ways to make a crude, though working, compass out of items you might have on your person. And there are other methods to find navigational directions based on the positions of the sun, moon, or stars. But if you are not absolutely sure of your skills in this area, it would be best to carry a compass.

Third, another vitally important tool is a map. There are many options here, such as topographic maps and others that will give relevant information about the area you are in. But again, you must know how to read your map and be familiar with the symbols and graphing that may be on it. When used in conjunction with a compass, a map is the ticket home. A GPS (global positioning system) device is also very handy and can be an invaluable tool for survival. It can have all the navigational aids and information you may need to get out alive — *but* it is *not* foolproof. First, you have to know how to use it properly. Second, it has to be loaded with pertinent information about your area. Third, and most importantly, you must have batteries! Many of the high-tech devices that are available today are real lifesavers — but when the batteries die, you die!

Fourth, a must-have piece of equipment for survival is a fire-starting source. This could be waterproof/strike-anywhere matches, a lighter, or a fire-starting tool or kit of one kind or another. The key is that it must be reliable, and once again, you must be proficient with it. Fire keeps you warm in the cold, gives illumination at night, can boil water to drink, can cook food to eat, can dry wet clothes, can signal for help, and can be used for a host of other survival chores. Along with a fire source, though, you must have the know-how to build a fire properly in the first place and be able to keep it going in a variety of conditions.

Fifth, a light source, such as a flashlight or headlamp, can be a tool of inestimable worth in wilderness survival, especially in a situation where you need to navigate through the woods or search for something, or someone, after dark. A lot of more civilized folks have no idea how absolutely, monumentally dark it can get in the woods at night, especially when there is cloud cover. It is a paralyzing blackness that can be extremely danger-ous to try to stumble around in and through. As I pointed out earlier, fire can certainly be used for illumination, but taking it with you isn't always the easiest and most productive thing in the world — and making an effective torch isn't quite as easy as it looks in the movies. Not to mention, if that torch goes out suddenly, you're in big trouble, mister! There are countless mod-els of flashlights available, so get a good one — and be darn sure you have additional, readily accessible, batteries and bulbs.

Sixth on the list is extra food. If you have a long way to go to reach safety and do not have the equipment or know-how to acquire proper nutrition from plant, animal, or other natural food sources that are in the area, then you had better have at least some form of nourishment to rely on. Lugging a cumber-some backpack full of chow around is certainly not the idea here. There are all kinds of options available today for nutrient-dense, compact, nonperishable (to a certain degree) food sources that you can take along for backup on wilderness outings. Things such as various "nutrition bars," dehydrated foods, and MREs (meals ready to eat) are good choices.

Contrary to popular and rather comical TV commercials, foods like beef jerky are not the best option for survival food.

While having a quality protein source is extremely important for longer, extended stays in the wilderness in order to maintain muscle mass and strength, it takes lots of water to digest meat, and this is not good when your water might be limited in the first place. That being the case, for short-term situations, foods chock-full of carbohydrates (notice the second half of the word here: "hydrate") and foods high in fat will provide the most energy and the highest caloric intake to fuel your bodily furnace most effectively for survival. If you're worried about maintaining your "no-carb" diet and refuse to eat such foods, then guess what? You're dead, buddy!

Seventh, extra clothes, or at least (and more importantly) an emergency space blanket or large trash bags (which can be filled with natural forms of insulation), will keep you warm and protected from the elements. When the temperature plummets, or the winds pick up, or the snow/ice/rain comes, your predicament can become miserable, and quite easily life-threatening, if you are not properly prepared. An extra layer of suitable clothes, an emergency blanket, or a trash bag filled with warm pine needles may be all you need to make it through the night. It can be the thin layer that saves your life. You might be exceptionally uncomfortable, but hey, it's better than being dead!

Eighth, and another must-have item for survival, is a first-aid kit. Cuts, infections, searing pain, gaping wounds, broken bones, ripped tendons, and venomous stings and bites are all part of the "great" outdoors. Having a good first-aid kit and a knowledge of basic first-aid skills can save life and limb. There are all manner of first-aid kits on the market today: some are very large and thorough, while others are quite small and rather worthless, really. First aid is an exceptionally important subject, and it is much too lengthy to go into appropriate depth here. So I'll simply suggest that you purchase a good manual, do your homework, and get a kit that will work for you and be of the most constructive use for the conditions you may encounter.

Ninth, and also extremely important, is a good knife or compact multi-tool. When we think of a "survival knife," images from *Rambo* movies may pop into our head, but don't forget: they are just movies. A good knife for survival purposes is one that has a "full-tang" construction — which means that the handle and blade are one piece, made from the same steel. This style of knife ensures that the handle will not break off during heavy, rugged use. The knife must also be of manageable size. A two-foot-long, head-chopping, hippopotamus-spearing blade is worthless for most survival tasks. You must be able to do everything from intricate notch cutting and careful fabric repair to gutting a deer and skinning a hide with the survival knife; an oversized blade makes these more delicate tasks very cumbersome.

Along with a good-quality knife (and a sharpening stone or two), a pocket multi-tool is another excellent piece of equipment to have handy in survival situations. It can aid you in nearly everything, from cutting wire to fixing broken gear, and from removing a splinter to opening cans. Such a tool is often easier to use and far more effective for certain survival tasks than a single, large knife blade. There are many good survival knives and multi-tools out there. So, as I've been saying, do some homework, read lots of reviews, talk to trustworthy folks, and check around before making a purchase that your life may depend upon.

And finally, *tenth*, you should have some sun/eye protection. This is one of those items that might not be the most important thing in a given situation — or at another time, it could be *the* most important thing. In windy, sandy, or snow-covered terrain where the sunlight and UV rays are excruciatingly intense, the lack of proper eye protection can render you blind. And then the rest of your survival skills and gear will be pretty much worthless, and the only thing you will have to look forward to is the pearly gates of heaven — or some even more intense heat from the fires of hell! How about that?

Along with sun protection for your eyeballs, skin protection is also extremely important while in those particular settings. That being the case, a bottle of maximum-protection sunscreen and a little tube of lip balm should also be in your survival pack.

Though these 10 things are of the utmost importance, and are mentioned on the list of "essential gear" from virtually all the sources I've gathered over the years, there are a few other items that some might put on this list in place of one of the others: things like an emergency whistle; a watertight, stainless-steel canister to use when boiling water or cooking food (which, by the way, is also handy for storing survival-kit items); Ziplock bags; light-gauge wire for making snare traps; needles; pen and paper; duct tape; a signaling mirror; and a stash of nylon cord. All of these additional items could certainly be essential to surviving a particular situation. As I have pointed out, the usefulness of some of these articles will depend on the area you will be in, so I suggest that you sit down and carefully prioritize them before your next outing.

It would be downright foolish to run off on a wild adventure without being fully prepared for the best — *and the worst* — that might come your way. Just a little extra planning, a few extra bucks, and a rather minuscule investment of study and practice time are all it takes to ensure that you'll be alive and kicking when another opportunity for outdoor adventure comes your way.

There is nothing heroic about being stupid.

The Spiritual Journey

As important as it is to be prepared for the journeys and perils of life, and as much as one may seriously pursue such wise preparations, it continually baffles me how so many in our world go through the adventures, and misadventures, of life without proper *spiritual* preparation. Many of us have no idea how to spiritually survive. What's even more alarming is that such a multitude of humanity does not even recognize the need for it. The journey of life is short, and one accident or slipup can bring that journey to a fatal end. The journey of eternity, however, is much longer — and a spiritual slipup might not only alter the course of our earthly journey, but carry over into eternity as well.

A grim part of being a priest is witnessing tragic death on a fairly regular basis. On more than one occasion, I've seen hardened, rebellious, godless men fall to their knees, sobbing and begging God for mercy, as they crouch down next to their freshly deceased spouse, child, parent, or friend. As the uncovered body of their loved one lies on the cold hospital bed in the emergency room, with tubes going everywhere, and the ominous sound of a flat-line heart monitor ringing like a sustained funeral knell, the reality of death is undeniable. For such individuals, when the once warm and tender hand of the only source of love and support in their life turns frigid and blue, and the once comforting eyes become glazed with expired mortality, there is no denying the reality that earthly life will end.

Death will come to you, and death will come to me. Then what? The answer to that question is a long and tedious one. It's a journey in and of itself, a journey of faith.

As a man of Christian faith, I believe and know that my life here on earth is the testing ground as to where I will spend eternity. If I have shared my life intimately with God here on earth, and lived according to his word and his will, then I will spend my eternal life with him in heaven. If I have continually, consciously, kicked God out of my life and pursued a life of sin and destruction, that, too, carries over into eternity: a little something known as hell — the absence of God — which is the most painful, horrific thing in the universe, yet a place and a state of soul that many purposely journey toward.

St. Paul reminds us:

> For we know that if the earthly tent we live in is
> destroyed, we have a building from God, a house not made

with hands, eternal in the heavens. Here indeed we groan, and long to put on our heavenly dwelling, so that by putting it on we may not be found naked. For while we are still in this tent, we sigh with anxiety; not that we would be unclothed, but that we would be further clothed, so that what is mortal may be swallowed up by life. He who has prepared us for this very thing is God, who has given us the Spirit as a guarantee.

So we are always of good courage; we know that while we are at home in the body we are away from the Lord, for we walk by faith, not by sight. We are of good courage, and we would rather be away from the body and at home with the Lord. So whether we are at home or away, we make it our aim to please him. For we must all appear before the judgment seat of Christ, so that each one may receive good or evil, according to what he has done in the body. (2 Cor 5:1-10)

You see, our home is not here on earth; the home we are called to is the kingdom of heaven. And to get to that kingdom, to make it back home, we must, as St. Paul said, "walk by faith, not by sight." This spiritual walk, this journey of faith, can be far more harrowing than a journey to the top of Mt. Everest. The dangers that await us on the road through life into eternity are "legion" (in more ways than one!). At every step of the way, there are slippery slopes, deep crevasses, and thin ice that cracks under the weight of temptation. When our footing becomes insecure and our grip weakens from lack of divine trust, we can easily fall into grave danger. When we're spiritually malnourished, the quest to the summit is never reached; we only continue to backslide with every passing day.

If we fail to protect our vision along the quest, we will be blinded by the harmful rays of materialism, secularism, and relativism. Our vision will be limited to the natural, the finite, and the mortal, only seeing the ordinariness and ungodliness of life, instead of seeing the supernatural and the infinite, knowing the extraordinariness and sacredness of life. We accept the facade, the illusions, and the blatant lies of our politically correct prophets of the day.

Our pilgrimage toward heaven can be plenty more dangerous than trying to make it out of the depths of the Amazon jungle. At every turn, there are venomous fangs waiting to inject us with sin. And when sickened and paralyzed by sin, we become easy prey for the larger, more formidable beast of vice. In the jungle of life, we may try to quench our thirst with the cool waters of cultural comforts, but we come to find that the waters are toxic, and rot us from the inside out. We may try to satisfy our aching hunger with the appealing plants of societal pleasures that are all around, but upon their consumption, we find they only give way to indignant retching and the wasting away of heart and soul.

Yes, the journey through life constantly reminds us of its earthly end: death. Our days are indeed numbered. And no matter what paths we've trod, no matter what roads we've walked, and no matter what mountains we've climbed, they all lead to the same end. At the end of the journey, we will all stand before God in judgment. At that time, nothing will be hidden. All will be revealed, which may be good, or not so good. The consequences of the choices we've made, or did not make, will become as plain as the noonday sun.

Thankfully, Christ is the one who has informed us well in advance of the consequences of both sin and righteousness. As we've already covered, the consequences of sin are death and destruction. The consequences of righteousness are life, love, and truth. These consequences affect us now, and into our life to come. But the good news is that our God has certainly not left us without his guidance as we journey into eternity. He has given us all we need to make it safely home. He has bestowed upon us the essential tools, skills, and knowledge for spiritual survival.

But it's up to us to gather those items, to practice those skills, and to put them to good use.

Spiritual Survival

The first step in our spiritual survival is to make sure we're on the right path. "And which one is that?" you ask. Our Lord tells us in Matthew's Gospel:

> "Enter by the narrow gate; for the gate is wide and the way is easy, that leads to destruction, and those who enter by it are many. For the gate is narrow and the way is hard, that leads to life, and those who find it are few." (Mt 7:13-14)

We can tell if we are on this more difficult, sanctified, challenging path by simply looking at the fruit our life is producing. You guessed it: the fruit we produce in life should be "good" — that is, it should help us fulfill the purpose for which we were created. And as we know, the purpose for which we were created is to know, love, and serve God, and to cherish and promote the gifts of life, love, and truth, which all have their fulfillment in him. If the fruits of your life are destruction, hate, and reveling in the lies of our culture, then you can be sure that you are way off the right path.

Now let's have a look at the essential tools for spiritual survival. We've already covered most of these earlier in this book (and I've covered the rest in my other books), so much of this will be a review — and a last-ditch effort to stress the vital, extreme importance of these things.

Just as water is absolutely essential for physical life, so the grace of God is absolutely essential for spiritual life. Grace is the nourishing, sustaining life of God within us, which we receive through things like the reception of the sacraments and prayer. It is friendship with the Almighty. Grace is a free and undeserved gift that God gives us to live out his will, with strength, courage, and love. It sanctifies us and helps us to develop in the ways of virtue, and to leave behind the ways of vice. Grace assists us in transforming our life into God's beautiful masterpiece. Grace enables our conscience to become more active in guiding us through those confusing and tempting paths that we sometimes travel. Grace makes us much more aware of things we should be doing — and of things we should be avoiding at all costs.

While a compass points us in the right direction, a properly formed conscience directs our thoughts and actions toward virtuous living. Our conscience is a great gift that God has given us. It is an imperative tool that we use to avoid sin, and it helps us decide to do the right thing. However, if our conscience is not properly formed, it is useless: it simply becomes a matter of making decisions based on our feelings, which often deceive us, rather than on the objective truth of right and wrong as God has revealed it to us.

Having an ill-formed conscience is like being color-blind. As our eyes have deteriorated, or lost their ability to perceive true color, a light may begin to look green, while in reality, it's actually red — and when we run that red light due to misperception, we get smashed by the oncoming traffic.

Sin also plays a big part in the use of our conscience. The more sin we have in our life — and the longer we go without recognizing it, repenting of it, and confessing it — the more our conscience is disintegrated and rendered powerless. Thus, we can see the vital importance of a properly formed conscience, which results from a three-step process of informing, reforming and conforming.

We *inform* our conscience by being taught right from wrong. This usually (hopefully) takes place, for the most part, when we are children. Our parents, teachers, priests, etc., help us to learn good from evil, and to strive for the good. It is also, in most cases, a rather natural process. That "little voice in the back of our heads" keeps us on the right path, if we've learned to listen to it. It's not just a one-time thing, though. We continue to inform our conscience all our life by staying up-to-date on the ethical and moral issues of our current time, and by paying attention and seeking to truly understand the teachings of Christ and his Church.

We should never stop seeking the truth and striving for goodness as we go through life. It's important to do our homework and get our information from trustworthy, godly sources — *not* from your local Church-hating newspaper or jaded, biased news program.

To *reform* our conscience means to take personal responsibility for our decisions, which is a rare thing these days. Everybody is a victim, everybody has an excuse, and it's always somebody else's fault. The fact is, though, that nobody puts a gun to our head and *makes* us sin — if that were the case, it wouldn't be a sin. Though temptation certainly gets the best of us at times, *we* make the decision, it's our responsibility, and it's our job to face the atonal music that we've composed for ourselves by our poor decisions and selfishness.

Finally, we must *conform* our conscience. This is basically the process of constantly striving to do the will of God in our life. And the basic will of God is the same for all of us: it is to love God, love others, and avoid sin, which destroys that love. One of the greatest tools to keep ourselves in check — and to help us with the informing, reforming, and conforming of our conscience — is to *examine* our conscience on a regular basis: that is, to take into account if we have acted in accordance with our faith and with God's will, or not. It is a process of holding ourselves accountable, of keeping tabs on our decisions and actions, and of recognizing if we have truly strived for good, or if we have let ourselves fall into sin.

An examination of conscience can, and should, be done daily. It really doesn't take much time. It's simply a matter of taking a few moments, looking over our day, recognizing the good, identifying the not-so-good, and committing to willfully making improvements in those not-so-good areas.

While a good map will educate and inform us about where we are, where we have come from, and where we need to go, the Word of God and the teachings of the Church give us the knowledge we need for our spiritual journey and survival. There are a number of different translations of the Bible out there, and different faith traditions promote and use different versions. But the important thing is to get familiar with the teachings of Christ and his Church. As I said earlier, in Scripture we not only experience the living Word of God, but we also come to understand the history and revelation of God and his plan of salvation for all people.

The Bible is about truth, not necessarily scientific fact. It is the account of God speaking to us both directly and through events. If we read the Bible looking for scientific explanations of things and take everything literally (except for those parts that are supposed to be taken literally), then we miss the point. The Bible has to be read, interpreted, and understood within the historical and cultural contexts in which it was written. Without a thorough understanding of this, we can use a particular verse or story of the Bible to back up all kinds of ridiculous claims, and make all sorts of absurd and mistaken points, that have absolutely nothing to do with the purpose for which those verses were originally written. Personal interpretation is very dangerous!

That being said, when implementing a regimen of Scripture study, it's good to supplement it with a study guide or Scripture commentary from an authoritative (Church approved) source. Remember, the Bible as we know it is a product of the authority of the Church as established by Christ himself and guided by the Holy Spirit. Christianity is not a religion that is merely based on a book. The book (Bible) came from the Church, not the other way around.

As we need fire and light to survive in the wild, so we need the fire and the light of the Holy Spirit for the survival of our soul. As the Church tells us, "In the Old Testament the prophets announced that the Spirit of the Lord would rest on the hoped-for Messiah for his saving mission (cf. Is 11:2; 61:1; Lk 4:16-22)." Later, in the New Testament, we learn how "The descent of the Holy Spirit on Jesus at his baptism by John was the sign that this was he who was to come, the Messiah, the Son of God (cf. Mt 3:13-17; Jn 1:33-34). He was conceived of the Holy Spirit; his whole life and his whole mission are carried out in total communion with the Holy Spirit whom the Father gives him 'without measure' (Jn 3:34)" (CCC 1286).

So, we see that from the very beginning the Holy Spirit was at work, preparing the way for Christ, and dwelling with him during his earthly ministry. But it doesn't stop there. Jesus gave that same Holy Spirit to the apostles at Pentecost, which fired them up so that they were able to go out and proclaim the Gospel and perform many mighty works for God. As the apostles then continued to work tirelessly, and the Church began to grow, those who were baptized received that same gift of the Holy Spirit.

Specifically, the gifts that the Holy Spirit gives to us are *wisdom*, *understanding*, *right judgment* (counsel), *courage* (might), *knowledge*, *reverence* (piety), and *fear of the Lord*. We see reference to these gifts in the words of the Prophet Isaiah:

> There shall come forth a shoot from the stump of Jesse,
> and a branch shall grow out of his roots.
> And the Spirit of the LORD shall rest upon him,
> the spirit of wisdom and understanding,
> the spirit of counsel and might,
> the spirit of knowledge and the fear of the LORD,
> And his delight shall be in the fear of the LORD.
> (Is 11:1-3)

(As a "footnote" here, the ancient Greek and Latin translations of this passage read "piety" for "fear of the Lord," in the first occurrence, which gives us our traditional seven gifts.)

As we learn to use and implement these gifts of the Holy Spirit more and more, we begin to see and experience the 12 fruits of the Holy Spirit. These 12 fruits (which are fairly self-explanatory) are charity, joy, peace, patience, kindness, goodness, generosity, gentleness, faithfulness, modesty, self-control, and chastity. Using the gifts of the Holy Spirit to their fullest, and sharing and experiencing the fruits they produce, lead to genuine holiness of life, a deeper friendship with God, and the spiritual backbone we need for survival.

As we've seen, we need protection from the elements in order to survive, whether it be extra clothes, an emergency blanket, or various sun-protection items. Naturally, we also need protection for our soul. The greatest protection of all, besides being in God's good grace and being constantly filled with the Holy Spirit, is the protection we get in numbers. Just as certain species of animals gather to stay safe, so also our gathering as a community of faith aids in our spiritual protection. As our Lord tells us in Matthew's Gospel: "For where two or three are gathered in my name, there am I in the midst of them" (Mt 18:20).

It's in our fellowship that we learn from one another, support one another, strengthen one another, forgive and heal one another, and love one another. No man is an island — but when we think we are, we remain lost on that island, in grave danger of spiritual death. God knows how important gathering as a community is for our spiritual survival, and that's why he *commands* us to keep his day holy. That's why Jesus *commanded* his followers to "*Do this* in memory of me" (emphasis added). So, in other words, get your butt to church and stop making excuses! Sacrificing one measly hour a week to come together as God's people, to say thank you for the gift of our salvation, which was purchased by the blood of Christ, is not asking too much. It's nothing compared to the sacrifice Jesus has made for you!

When you're stuck in the wild with no quick way out, you're going to need food to strengthen you for the rigorous road ahead. Likewise, we all need food for our spiritual journey. For Catholics, our spiritual food is the Eucharist, which is the "source and summit" of our faith, and of our lives as Christians. We believe that Jesus truly becomes present in the consecrated bread and wine at the celebration of Mass, that the bread and wine truly become the Lord's body and blood, though still remaining hidden in the appearance of mere food.

We get this belief and doctrine from Jesus himself, as recalled in the Eucharistic Prayer at Mass. When Jesus was with his disciples, on the night before he died, he took the bread, broke it, and gave it to them and said:

> Take this, all of you, and eat it:
> this *is* my body which will be given up for you.
>   (emphasis added)

When the supper ended, Jesus took the cup of wine, gave God thanks and praise, and gave the cup to his disciples and said:

> Take this, all of you, and drink from it:
> this *is* the cup of my blood,
> the blood of the new and everlasting covenant.
> It will be shed for you and for all
> so that sins may be forgiven.
> Do this in memory of me. (emphasis added)

These are powerful words. It's during these "words of institution" (as they are called) that the change from bread and wine into the body and blood of Christ takes place. Jesus was very direct and clear with what he said. Notice that he did not say "This *represents* my body and blood" or "This *symbolizes* my body and blood," but rather "this *is* my body and blood." In the Gospel of John, Jesus says this:

> "Truly, truly, I say to you, unless you eat the flesh of the Son of man and drink his blood, you have no life in you; he who eats my flesh and drinks my blood has eternal life, and I will raise him up at the last day. For my flesh is food indeed, and my blood is drink indeed. He who eats my flesh and drinks my blood abides in me, and I in him." (Jn 6:53-56)

> "The bread which I shall give for the life of the world is my flesh." (Jn 6:51)

These are hard words for many today, just as they were for those in Jesus' time. John's Gospel goes on to tell us that many of those who followed Jesus could not accept this teaching and went back to their former way of life. It's important to note that, here again, while some of his followers started to leave, Jesus didn't try to stop them by yelling out, "Wait! I didn't *actually* mean that it's *really* my flesh and blood! Come back!" No, Jesus simply asked those who remained, "Will you also go away?" (Jn 6:67). Jesus did not compromise or speak symbolically about the nature of the Eucharist, and neither should we.

After receiving Jesus in the Eucharist, we are filled with his grace and thus are empowered, nourished, and strengthened to go out into the world and put his words into practice. It is food for the body and, more importantly, for the soul. It is truly the "Bread of Life."

(For you non-Catholics, there is a lot more to it than this. So, if you're interested in finding out more, check out my book *Meat & Potatoes Catholicism* for a more detailed explanation. Other great places for information on what we Catholics *really* believe and practice — and why — include these Internet sites: *www.CatholicBridge.com* and Catholic Answers at *www.Catholic.com*.

Just as a first-aid kit is essential to heal wounds and treat injuries that we may sustain while trying to survive a particular predicament, so it is forgiveness that brings healing to our souls and binds up the wounds that we inflict on ourselves, on others, and on God by our sins. There is tremendous healing power in saying "I'm sorry" and "I forgive you" — and really meaning it. The heartfelt speaking of those few words can remove a mountain of pain, can dry up an ocean of ill will, and can wash away a laundry-load of grudges and hatred.

The practice of forgiveness — and acceptance of it — isn't always easy, but it is that which helps us survive the deep cuts of the divisions of pride and jealousy. It binds the broken bones caused by greed and wrath. Forgiveness soothes the interior turmoil of gluttony and lust. Just like the aftermath of a deep gash caused by the slip of a rusty blade, so the scars of our spiritual wounds may always remain. But forgiveness is what truly heals the damage underneath, and it restores and strengthens us and others to trudge forward on our journey home. Don't forget: "The measure you give will be the measure you get" (Mt 7:2; also see Mk 4:24 and Lk 6:38) — and, Lord knows, we all need a good measure of forgiveness from the Almighty. It's far beyond *vital* for our spiritual survival!

Last, but not least: Just as we need a good, sturdy knife or some basic tools to make ends meet while stranded in the wilds, likewise we need some essential spiritual tools. We discussed a few of them earlier, but one of the most important is communication with God — that is, prayer. I discussed prayer quite a bit in *Hunting for God, Fishing for the Lord*, so I won't repeat it all.

Basically, prayer is our lifeline to the Lord. There are lots of ways to pray, but the heart of prayer is simply, consciously, spending time in God's presence — communicating with him, listening to him, being with him. We can engage in a devotional workout while in prayer, or we can do absolutely nothing, remaining quiet and listening while in prayer. Prayer comes in many forms and is practiced in many ways. And, no doubt, one person's method of prayer can be quite different from another's.

The bottom line, and the most important thing of all, is to simply do it! Just as we have to make time for our other relationships in life, so we have to *make* time for God.

It's our communication with God — our prayer — that signals him for help, that asks him for the courage to follow our spiritual compass, and that petitions him for the wisdom to read and understand the map he has given us. Prayer makes us more prepared to be filled with the fire and the light of the Holy Spirit. It gives us the thirst for the waters of God's grace, and it makes us realize that we need to seek his presence in the presence of others, who are made in the divine image and likeness.

Summing Up: It Is God Who Tracks Us!

Well, we've covered a lot in this chapter, and in this book as a whole. We've tracked God using philosophical, theological, scientific, and scriptural methods. And we've hunted for God in creation and fished for the Lord in many wonderful outdoor adventures, which I've been so blessed to be able to share with you. I hope to bring you more in the future.

Throughout this book, we've stared vice square in the eye, exposed it for what it is, and learned how to take it on with the power of virtue. We've also learned the basics of what we need for physical and, more importantly, spiritual survival.

But you know what? As much as we might think that our spiritual journey consists of us seeking God, the reality is that it is *God* who seeks you and me. God is tracking us! He looks for you through the tender eyes of a newborn babe. He reaches out to you through the love and wisdom of the elderly. He calls to you through the warm regards of a dear friend. As fast as you race down the path of life, God is on your trail, waiting for you to be still for a while, and to take a rest so that you might recognize his presence. The Almighty longs to see your footprints in his Church, and to see the tracks of your eyes upon his word. The Lord has his ear to the ground, waiting to hear the beat of your heart pound with love for him. He speaks to you in the wind and the rain, He displays his wonders to you in his creation, and warms your cold, tired blood with the life-giving rays of his Son.

While you pound your feeble brain with unanswerable questions and seek truth in the dust, he — the Way, the Truth, and the Life — is standing by to cool your burning heart in the shadow of his omnipotent presence. My prayer for you, my friend, is that you will no longer be satisfied with just your vision, but that you will truly learn to see. As you continue to hunt for God, know that it is he who hunts for you. So do not be afraid to let him capture your heart and soul.

Until next time ...

APPENDIX

A Message From Father Classen on the Ethics of Hunting and Fishing

I'M WELL AWARE that some will be upset, and perhaps scandalized, by the notion of a priest who not only actively hunts and fishes, but who also passionately promotes it. I do get rather amusing hate-mail from time to time in which the usually anonymous author emphatically asks, "How can you, a man of God, kill his creatures?"

My response is, ultimately, one word: food. While many Americans do their "hunting" at the grocery store, we in the outdoors community do it in the woods and on the waters.

Many misguided, uneducated folks believe that hunters and fishermen exist only to rape the land of its resources and kill animals for the "sport" of it. Personally, I don't consider hunting or fishing a "sport" at all. I, like millions of others, venture into the outdoors to spend time with God, family, and friends, while being surrounded by the beauty of our Lord's creation — and, yes, at times I respectfully harvest food from that creation to sustain my life and feed others, as it was intended.

Those who truly love the outdoors have a deep respect for all of creation and take an active role in keeping our precious resources alive and healthy for future generations. Here in the United States, millions of acres of wildlife refuge, and the very existence of certain species of animals, are the direct result of funding and implementation by hunters and fishermen. I would dare say that no other group cares more about these things than the hunting and fishing community. And it's not out of selfishness so that we can have "more things to kill," as some would say, but rather, our concern flows from a hyper-awareness of the intrinsic life-sustaining and soul-nourishing value of these great gifts.

No people are more intimately connected to the wild world than outdoors men and women. We don't just admire and cherish these gifts but also responsibly practice hands-on management of them for future generations — and this is why the vast majority of hunters and fishing men and women have the utmost respect for their quarry and the land that supports it. This is also why we only take what we need or can give to others. There are programs in place throughout the United States in which hunters are able to harvest deer (and other game animals) from severely overpopulated areas (a deadly situation for all) and give the meat to the poor. As the Lord fed the 5,000 with fish and bread, so we feed the hungry with venison. Meanwhile, some well-known organizations that claim to be concerned with "humane" causes do nothing for the promotion of the humane treatment of human beings (like feeding hungry families), who are made in the image and likeness of God.

Please keep this in mind: a governing rule of life on earth is that something must die for something else to live. Hunters and fishermen know firsthand the price their food has paid; thus, they foster a sense of the sacred in what they do and what they eat. A true hunter understands the paradox of taking life. It is sad to see a beautiful animal die. As I said earlier, it is not fun to watch the spark of life dwindle away from a creature's eyes, knowing that one is directly responsible for its death. But along with this comes the satisfaction and sense of joy in being an active participant in the cycle of life and having harvested an animal or fish with a humane kill, true respect, sacred reverence, and deep gratitude to God. Other natural predators are not so thoughtful or kind — and neither is Mother Nature, who "thins the herd" with disease and starvation. As the spark of life fades from our quarry's eyes, it enlightens and sustains the spark in ours. Death gives way to life in more ways than one. As I also said earlier, if a hunter's or fisherman's killing only gives way to death, then it's time to quit. These are the principles I — and all serious outdoors men and women — live by.

Regarding the death of animals, here are a few other things to consider:

- If you buy meat, fish, or poultry from the market, then you have had a hand in the death of those creatures.
- If you are a vegetarian and buy your vegetables from mainstream grocery stores, you are still responsible for the death of animals. Why? Because, nationwide, hundreds of thousands of animals are killed in the process of growing food. Some are eradicated because of their destruction of crops, and others are killed accidentally as a result of harvesting methods.
- If you feed your dog or cat the usual store-bought pet food, here again you have had a hand in killing animals. One of the main ingredients in dog/cat food is *meat* by-products. (And don't forget that our furry friends are natural hunters, too!)
- If you live in a new house in the suburbs, you may be responsible for the death of animals in another way: your new home has destroyed their habitat and displaced them.

The bottom line is that every living creature on earth, with few exceptions, must seek out (hunt), kill, and eat other living things: plants, fruits, and all forms of vegetation; bugs, birds, fish, and other animals. This is a simple fact of life on earth. To deny it, to reject it, or to otherwise turn a blind eye to the reality of the food chain is pure ignorance.

In Sacred Scripture, we see clearly that mankind was created in the "image and likeness" of God. We were made the stewards of creation — and with that responsibility, we were given dominion over animals, along with the command to care for and use them properly. Throughout the Bible, we read about the killing of animals by various means — including hunting and fishing — for food, clothing, and sacrifice. We learn that Jesus ate fish and declared all foods (including meat) as "clean" (see Mk 7:14-19 and Acts 10:9-16). As a Jew, Jesus would have also eaten lamb. Contrary to the ridiculous propositions of "animal-rights" groups, Jesus was certainly not a vegetarian. And don't forget that his first disciples were, in fact, fishermen!

Hunting and fishing are as natural and healthy as breathing the air that keeps us alive. There is simply no reason to apologize for becoming an active, respectful, considerate participant in the food chain and putting food on the table, and in the freezer, by one's own efforts.

About the Author

FATHER JOSEPH CLASSEN, ordained to the priesthood in 2003, is associate pastor at St. Margaret Mary Alacoque Church in St. Louis, Missouri. He holds a Bachelor of Arts degree in philosophy from St. Louis University and a Master of Divinity degree from the Kenrick School of Theology.